All Things Girl

Truth for Teens

The *All Things Girl* Series, along with other excellent fiction and non-fiction books, is published by Bezalel Books in Waterford, MI

www.BezalelBooks.com
www.ATGSeries.com
www.TeresaTomeo.com

Printed in the United States of America

ISBN 978-0-9823388-3-4
Library of Congress Control Number 2009934222

Our special thanks to the following sisters-in-the-Lord who have shared their passions with us through their offerings to this work:

Joan L. Kelly, Catholic author (*My Big Feet, Hiding the Stranger* series, and *Lonny the Lizard*) and avid gardener has graciously given us the material for "How Does Your Garden Grow?"

Harriet Sabatini, Catholic author (*Joseph's Hands* – English and Spanish – and *Isabel's Sister*) and avid equestrian also runs Marygate in Alabama has allowed us to delve into her wonderful cache of inspirational articles for "Learning from All God's Creatures."

Mary Ceccanese who shares her life lessons and enthusiasm for living as a financially responsible Catholic woman and who painstakingly edited this work so that it would give glory to God. We are truly indebted to her.

In Christ,
Teresa Tomeo
Molly Miller
Monica Cops
Cheryl Dickow

You Are
Here
for a
Reason

Every person is unique. There are no doubles. God created only one you. He created you in His image and likeness. This is what gives you the dignity of a person, different from the animals. You are not just some*thing* but SOME*ONE*. It is so important for you as a young woman to understand and embrace your God given dignity, your worth. As a teenager, do you have any idea how much you are worth? The *Catechism of the Catholic Church* (*CCC*) teaches that the human person is "the only creature on earth that God has willed for its own sake." This means that God's love for you is so immense, that He created you to share in His own life. Each one-of-a-kind person is made to know, love and serve God in this life and to be happy with Him forever in the next life. No other creature has this privilege.

You Have a Unique and Immeasurable Worth!

So, how does this affect you? As a person, God created you for a purpose. Have you ever thought of that? This life is like a trip; you're just passing through. Your final destination is Heaven to be with God forever. How are you going to go through life and get to Heaven? Think of a bus trip from Florida to Michigan. You have several options. Bus #98 travels west through all the southern states and then turns north in California, goes east when it arrives in Seattle. It's a trip with a very long detour but you do eventually arrive in Michigan after about a week. Bus #76 has a new driver who doesn't know the route very well. He starts off on the right highway but then takes a wrong turn and starts driving northwest. He never makes it to Michigan because he is hopelessly lost and refuses to ask directions. Bus #44 travels north

through Georgia, Tennessee, Kentucky, Ohio and reaches Michigan in a relatively short time. It was a long trip, but along the way the scenery was pretty and there were interesting people you met on the way. The Catholic Church is like Bus #44. It offers the most direct path to Heaven because She possesses the fullness of truth.

The Catholic Church teaches that there are three simple steps that will allow you to fulfill your purpose of eternal life with God.

They Are to Know, Love and Serve God.

Let's take a closer look on how to accomplish this.

To know God

This takes effort on your part. If you have very little idea of who God is, start with reading the Bible, especially the New Testament. The *CCC* is a great resource that uses Scripture and other references to teach the Catholic faith and answer questions.

Seek out a priest and talk with him about your quest to know God. His entire life is dedicated to helping others get to Heaven.

If you are blessed to have a mom and dad that are practicing their faith, they are a great resource. You get to know God the same way you have gotten to know your friends. You have conversations – you share things and do things together. It is the same with God. By talking to Him, praying, going to Mass and learning about Him, you will get to know God in an intimate way.

To love God

To love God is to know God. Once you get to know Him through the above ways, you will begin to love the Triune

God – the Father, God the Son and God the Holy Spirit. This is because God is love.

To serve God

To serve God falls into place because knowing and loving God, you will want to share Him and that is serving Him. No matter what it is, something done for another person is done for God Himself. Again, it takes a lifetime to know, love and serve God, but it is truly a life of joy. That's not to say you won't experience difficulties, but you will have peace and joy through your experiences.

God's Gift to You is Your Dignity and Your Worth.

There was a girl named Mary who was a skinny, funny looking girl her entire life. All through grade school she was teased mercilessly. She didn't even have one friend to turn to for comfort. This continued into high school. Mary never really understood her dignity and worth – these precious gifts from God.

One day after graduation, Mary's mother found her in bed, Mary had lost hope in the future and thought that suicide was the best answer. Somewhere along the line, she never realized her inherent worth as a human person and felt despair.

A seemingly happy, popular young girl might feel the same sort of despair as Mary.

Oftentimes – more often than not – we just don't know what is going on in a person's mind and how she is feeling in the depths of her heart. People are fragile and ought to be treated with love and kindness, even when they don't seem to deserve such nice treatment.

You are so loved by God. He wants you to make a difference in your space, in your time. He has given you gifts and talents unlike any other person. The popular culture today wants you to think that unless you are thin, have the perfect skin, hair and face that you are not as important as those who do have that. What a lie! No matter what you look like, what size clothing you wear, whether or not you are smart, or rich, you have the worth of a rare jewel. How Mary's mother and family wish today that she had believed this. Mary didn't realize her worth and, consequently, her purpose in life here on earth was thwarted. Though we don't make a judgment about her eternal soul, we can say that she didn't finish her life on earth as God intended.

As a young woman, you have your entire life ahead. It is a mystery, a gift that has yet to be opened. Realize that you are made in God's own image and you have a unique purpose. It is important for you to love yourself in a healthy way.

Can you look in the mirror and tell yourself, "I am one of a kind! I have gifts and abilities! My life is worthwhile! I am good?" If this is hard for you, girl, you've got to work on this.

If you have "friends" who don't build you up, find new ones. A friend really should challenge you to be your best and not make you sink into feelings of despair or jealousy or anger.

And always remember to be the sort of friend who brings out the best in others! Lift others up – never push them down.

Here are some tips:

✞ Keep your media, music and conversations positive.

✞ Make sure the conversations you have with yourself are also good ones!

> o Always remember that you can do more damage to yourself than others if you let negative messages play over and over in your head.

> o Whenever you get a negative thought about yourself, immediately replace it with a good one. It does seem cheesy, but the brain is like a computer – whatever you put in, is what comes out.

> o Learn to truly and completely love who you are, just as God created you, while learning how to become all that God wants you to be.

✞ Make sure the conversations you have with others help them become better – not through tearing them down but through building them up.

✞ Make sure you are taking the time to build your prayer life.

✞ Take advantage of the Sacrament of Reconciliation if you are feeling overwhelmed, or burdened, by things you've done – like saying something mean about someone – or haven't done – like saying a kind word to someone who needed to hear it.

✞ Be loving in your home to your family. This will help you be a more positive, loving person outside of your home!

✞ See others as created by God so that you will see them with love. This is especially true for the ones who seem un-loveable.

✞ Do some journal writing that can help you "work things out" in a positive way.

Relationships

Girlfriends

There's nothing like a few good girlfriends to keep life interesting. But did you know that you don't need a lot of friends? A few first-class ones will do the trick!

One girl may make you laugh, one may be your confidant and advisor, and one may be your fashion stylist. Having just a few good girlfriends in a young woman's life can be priceless. There's an old saying that  quality is more important than quantity and that certainly applies to one's friends!

The bottom line on friends, though, is that they need to have the same goals for eternal life as you do. That's not  to say you can't have non-Christian friends, but your close pals need to reflect your values. A good friend wants the best for you and that is Heaven. The reverse is also true; you need to help those you love get there too.

When choosing friends, look up! Meaning, find those that are achieving the goals you want to achieve. Search out individuals that practice virtuous lives. Good friendships foster mutual growth and satisfaction. Reach out to the girls or guys like Mary, who have no one to befriend them. You may find that they have special things to offer you as a friend. Human  beings were created to be with others and to have relationships. No man is an island; we all need each other. When you observe someone like Mary, put yourself in her shoes and think about how you would feel if no one gave you the time of day.

Friends a Girl Needs

Prayerful Priscilla

She's there whenever you need prayer. When she promises to pray for you, you know you can count on her. Whatever you have on your mind, Priscilla has a prayer for it. If your family has experienced a tragedy, she'll pray with you at a moment's notice and the words will flow out of her mouth. When you are joyful and celebrating an accomplishment she's there with a beautiful prayer of thanksgiving. Every girl needs a Prayerful Priscilla as a friend.

Fun-Loving Fiona

She's the one who wants to go midnight sledding or comes up with crazy ideas for parties. Fiona doesn't take life too seriously and helps her friends enjoy life. She is the life of every party and in fact the party doesn't start until Fiona gets there. She wants everyone to have a good time and spreads the joy around. If your "crush" likes someone else, and you are feeling blue, Fiona will go to great pains to cheer you up. She'll show up at your door with five pounds of chocolate and Chinese takeout for a night of chick flicks. Now that's a friend!

Cassie the Coach

She's the one you go to for advice. Cassie is levelheaded and wise beyond her years. Cassie can handle any kind of "issue." She can help you sort out what kind of career you should strive for, how to fix problems with your friends, and what things are important. Cassie just knows how to put things in perspective. She will always have time for you to pour out your heart about anything. She never interrupts to tell you her problems but gives you all the time you need. She will encourage you and will be your cheerleader whenever you need it.

Stylin' Stella

She has it all going on with the hair, makeup and fashion. If you wanna know if something looks good on you, Stella's the one to ask. She wouldn't dream of letting you get a pair of jeans that makes your butt look big. Take her to the salon with you when you want a new "do." She'll know exactly what to tell the stylist, and then she'll supervise to make sure it's done right. Stella will tell you that you have a uni-brow and wax it for you. She'll go through your entire wardrobe and give you advice on how to make things look good. Everybody needs a Stella.

NOTE TO SELF: Because of the differences between men and women, women need to have girlfriends. A young woman shouldn't expect a young man to react to things the way a girlfriend would – God didn't create men and women the same. **God created men and women equal but different.** Men use fewer words a day than women. Females are often more emotional. Women are drawn to beauty in a way that men often are not. These attributes allow women to form deep relationships with one another.

What Sort of Friend Are You to Others?

Section 1 (Prayerful Priscilla)

✝ You are concerned about your friends' spiritual life
✝ You have a serious disposition
✝ You pray for your friends
✝ You are open about your faith
✝ You are comfortable praying aloud in public
✝ Spontaneous prayers come easy to you

Section 2 (Fun-Loving Fiona)

✝ You love to laugh and make others laugh
✝ You love social functions and parties
✝ You plan most of your friends' weekends
✝ You love practical jokes
✝ You are creative and original in your ideas
✝ When you're around everyone's having fun

Section 3 (Coach Cassie)

✝ All your friends come to you for advice
✝ You are a good listener
✝ Solving problems comes easy to you
✝ You are an analytical thinker
✝ You are loyal and trustworthy
✝ You have goals and plans for your life

Section 4 (Stylin' Stella)

✝ You are good at putting colors and styles together
✝ You have artistic talents
✝ You like to keep up with fashion and hair style trends
✝ You always tell your friends the truth about how they look in their clothing
✝ You can put together a wardrobe on a limited budget
✝ You enjoy helping others look their best

Friendships have their ups and downs. The strong friendships grow better and more resilient when they make it through hard times. Not all friendships are meant to last a lifetime, though.

There are people who will come and go – for a reason or for a season – but Jesus will always be your friend.

There may be a time in your life when you have experienced backstabbing or jealousy with girls. These experiences hurt and, sadly, some young women grow to distrust other women as a result. Ladies, don't let these types of experiences keep you from experiencing good relationships with women.

Friendships with other women are irreplaceable and beautiful. Sadly, there will always be a "mean girl" in class, at work or in the neighborhood. Just make sure you're not the "mean girl" to others. If you check off anything from the following list, you have been or are a "mean girl." Realize your mistakes, go to confession and start again. You get further in life being nice, and even though it may seem like a lot of responsibility, you should always do your best to act like a daughter of the King – even when it feels impossible. God is good about giving grace when you need it and building a relationship with Him will always have great rewards.

The Mean Girl:

➢ Talks about others behind their backs
➢ Plans parties and events and discusses them in front of those who are not invited
➢ Tells others' secrets
➢ Won't stand up for her friends in front of the "popular people"
➢ Teases and then says she is kidding
➢ Starts rumors about others
➢ Ridicules others
➢ Pretends to be a friend and then turns against that person to further her own interests
➢ Uses technology to spread unflattering pictures or stories about others
➢ Uses others for her own purposes

There are a million reasons the mean girl could be insecure but here's a few:

➢ She struggles in school
➢ She has family issues
➢ She's afraid of not being the best or the prettiest
➢ She's jealous of something you have
➢ She doesn't like her looks or her figure

What you can do:

➢ Make sure you stand up for yourself and your friends
➢ Pray for the mean girl and consider ways in which you can be nice to her without sacrificing your own dignity or worth

This entire mean girl scenario has made many a girl miserable. In a nutshell, though, you can usually fix this problem by being assertive and compassionate. Of course, it's always best to talk to your parents if there is any physical abuse taking place or you feel you've done your best to handle it and that just hasn't worked.

But if you are experiencing the typical teasing, name calling, or ostracizing, you need to get a handle on it. The sooner you stand up for yourself, the sooner the mean girl and her followers will back off. Make sure you are prepared when she strikes and have some comebacks in mind. Practice them in your mind so that when the time comes, you'll be prepared. You have to let her know that you don't care what she thinks. The mean chick has to realize that you just won't put up with her junk. There's no need for violence, just say things firmly and passionately. Make sure, too, that your friends will stand up for you and that you all stick together. There is power in numbers and the mean girl knows it. If you think the mean girl is a friend, think again. Friends don't put each other down, embarrass each other, or try to outdo one another.

Ditch the mean girl and move on.

Forgotten Friends: The Communion of Saints

Oftentimes Catholic teens forget that there is a great source of friendships in our "communion of saints." Let's face it, we all need a friend who doesn't let us down and these saints, who are in the presence of God, can be just that to us! Just like you should call Jesus "friend," so should you remember that the communion of saints is a vast network of friends who are in heaven. They are the best sort of friends in that they have the ear of God and as long as you are acting selflessly and with great love, they are anxious to take your requests directly to Him. They can give you strength and courage and can help you live more joyfully while on earth.

So, the next time you feel like picking up your cell and making a call, or sending a text, how about conversing with one of your heavenly friends instead? You might be very glad you did!

The intercession of saints, "Being more closely united to Christ, those who dwell in heaven fix the whole Church more firmly in holiness... They do not cease to intercede with the Father for us, as they proffer the merits which they acquired on earth through the one mediator between God and men, Christ Jesus...So by their frequent concern is our weakness greatly helped."
CCC #956

Boys

Boys, boys, boys. It seems the movies, TV shows, and the culture idolizes "love" and a "passionate" relationship with the opposite sex. Everywhere you look you are getting the message that being sexually active before marriage is perfectly acceptable. But it isn't – it's wrong.

It is a serious sin, which cuts off your relationship with God. But what's a girl to do? How does a girl say "no" to an impure relationship, especially if she really likes a guy and is attracted to him?

Let's start with the purpose of dating. Dating is for those who are ready to get married. It is a time when a man and a woman get to know each other in order to see if they are compatible to marry. If you are not intending to marry anytime soon, it is best not to date but to have friendships and do things in groups. This is not a popular idea in this day and age where "hooking up" is all the rage. Many times teens get in over their heads because they "hook up" instead of forming meaningful, chaste relationships with the opposite sex. The passions are strong and if you're not careful, you can find yourself in intimate situations you are not prepared to handle.

In the "olden days" when sex was reserved for marriage, as it should really always be, male and female teens had fun together and got to know each other as people. They flirted at picnics, where all the family members were present, or they had dinner at one another's home. They attended dances that were chaperoned and they did things with whole groups of friends. You see it wasn't as if the "old" generation didn't have temptations; but, rather, they understood that temptations were something to be aware of and conquer.

Remaining pure, before marriage, was pretty much the norm and was seen as a good virtue. We'll look at virtues a little later in the book. Sadly, though, practicing virtues isn't all that popular nowadays. Young women who want to be chaste are in the minority and the culture doesn't hold up this virtue, but makes fun of it.

Yes, these are all challenges for you today. Lucky you, huh? Just keep in mind that it is near impossible to stick to your values and beliefs without God's help. That's why making a prayer plan and sticking to it is critical!

Dating should be discussed with your parents. They are to help and guide you during this time in your life. They didn't get to be the age they are at without being your age first. And it is ridiculous for you to think your parents didn't have the same sorts of problems you have now or that they can't relate. In fact, no one can help you more than your parents so don't shut them out of your life.

If you want to talk with your mom about some of the kinds of guys you know or think about, you should. Let her know ahead of time that you need some private time and she will make sure it happens. Moms are good about that.

Here's a list and some stories to share with her to get the conversation started. Or just read through it yourself and take some notes so that you are making good decisions about boys. You know what they say, "Knowledge is power!"

Typically there are certain "characters" out there in the dating world. Of course they are stereotypes and not every guy fits into a stereotype, but check it out and see if you recognize any of these guys:

The Bad Boy

He's the guy who likes to bend the rules and make his own. He's been in trouble with the law, maybe kicked out of school. He likes to experiment with drugs, drinking and sex. However, he appeals to nice girls sometimes. Women like to fix things and make everyone happy, so when a nice girl dates a Bad Boy she tries to change him and straighten him out.

There was a cute, smart girl named Caitlin who started dating a Bad Boy when she was a senior in high school. Greg was so handsome. He had spent his childhood in foster homes and she felt sorry for him. His mother and father fought, they were both alcoholics and Greg's father abused him. At sixteen Greg had dropped out of school and was working odd jobs between getting stoned. Caitlin had a traditional family with mom and dad married, was one of six kids and lived in a typical middle-class neighborhood. She knew her parents would not allow her to go out with Greg so she went behind their backs to be with him. Caitlin "fell in love" with Greg and wanted so much to help him change his life. The sad thing was, though, she was not strong enough to bring him "up" and so he brought her down to his level. They began to have an impure relationship. Caitlin moved out of her parents' home. She could not live with her sinfulness as long as she was under their roof. Soon Caitlin was pregnant. Her parents and family were devastated! The couple insisted on staying together and, luckily, they gave their child up for adoption.

During the pregnancy Caitlin and Greg stayed away from her family. She kept her parents completely out of the picture. They made their plans for adoption and went through the entire ordeal without parental support, by Caitlin's choosing. Her parents and family were heartbroken. After the pregnancy and adoption, Caitlin and Greg decided to get married. This caused even more grief because by this time Caitlin had rejected her childhood faith and left the Catholic Church. Her mother and father again experienced a knife in their hearts as they continued to watch their daughter take the wrong path. With a beginning like this, Caitlin's parents knew that she would experience a lot of pain and heartache. They could do nothing but stand by, pray and watch as their daughter made one mistake after another.

Soon after the wedding, there was "trouble in paradise" for Caitlin and Greg. Greg's drinking was causing fights between the couple. One night it became violent with Caitlin running from the apartment. Greg, intoxicated, got in his truck and began chasing her, nearly running her over. After this incident, Caitlin's parents begged her to leave him and get a civil annulment. She refused.

Five years later, Greg had gotten his GED and was working to become a plumber. Things seemed to have settled down and the couple seemed to the outside to be making it work. WRONG. Greg would always be from the wrong side of the tracks. Caitlin had "fixed" him as much as she could and now she had outgrown him. She was working in a career where she was with professionals. Greg would never fit in. Caitlin began to see other men behind his back. Eventually she left Greg.

To this day, she has the baggage of the child she gave up, and a divorce. How much anguish Caitlin caused herself and her family all because she dated a Bad Boy and tried to change him. It's never a good idea to date this kind of guy. They will bring you down to their level no matter how good your intentions are. Stay away from the BAD Boy!

The Bum

The Bum has some appeal to girls. Maybe he's cute or funny, or just plain fun to be around. Some girls fall for the Bum because they don't have enough confidence to do any better. This guy never has any money because he either doesn't work or spends it. This guy is characterized by not having much ambition, and may live at home with no intention of leaving the nest. If mom and dad pay his way he's happy. If you go out with the Bum, you better bring your own money because he won't be able to pay. Be prepared to sit at his house and watch movies. He won't be able to take you to a movie, to dinner, or dancing because he's always broke. He can't even afford to take you for a cup of coffee. It's not that a guy has to be rich to go out with, but the Bum is just plain lazy and that is a trait to stay away from! If you choose to stick with the Bum, you'll spend the rest of your life paying your way and his.

Once upon a time a college girl named Shari met the Bum at a summer job. He was so nice and accepted her for who she was. Shari was used to guys who didn't take her seriously and always wanted a physical relationship. The Bum was easygoing and didn't make these kinds of passes at her. Shari and the Bum dated for a while, that is if you call what they were doing "dating." They sat around watching movies on TV and ate junk food. Both of them put on a few pounds just hanging out together. Once in a while they were invited out with Shari's friends and the Bum never had any cash so she always had to pay. Shari liked talking about her career plans and what she was doing in college. The Bum never had much to say about that and he never talked about his own dreams and plans because he didn't have any. It became apparent to Shari that this relationship would never work out so she smartly, but kindly, ended the relationship.

The Octopus

The Octopus is the kind of guy that is fast with girls and has one thing in mind – SEX. He acts like a male dog after a female in heat. Of course this guy takes on many appearances. He may be smart, good-looking, athletic, ambitious, funny and easy to like. You won't know what he's really all about until you're alone with him. Then, in a split second, he's got at least eight hands and they're all over you. This guy doesn't like to be told "No." In fact he thinks "No" means "Yes." He actually thinks he has the right to touch whoever and whatever he pleases. Since he has so many hands, it can be hard to get away from him. The Octopus can actually be dangerous. Depending on the guy, the Octopus may force you into things you are not ready to do and don't want to do. This is the kind of guy who is capable of date rape.

Missy was a sophomore in college who liked to go to parties with her friends. She had always been a friendly girl and liked attention. One Saturday night at a fraternity party she spotted Joe, the cute guy she always saw in several of her classes. She had never been introduced to him so she decided to introduce herself. He seemed pleasant and they spent the evening talking and laughing. Missy's friends were ready to leave but she wanted to stay and spend more time with Joe. Joe told Missy he would be happy to get her home when the party broke up. When Joe finally brought Missy home, she didn't want things to end so she invited him into her home. One thing lead to another and soon Missy found herself in real trouble. Missy had never been with a guy who didn't respect her. She always went out with nice guys who didn't try things with her. Naively Missy assumed all guys were that way. Missy was in way over her head this time and with a guy she had just met. All she had meant to do was to kiss Joe and the next thing she knew, clothes were coming off! In the end Joe did not force Missy into intercourse. She had cried and begged him to stop because she was a virgin. The following day,

Missy was completely humiliated and never wanted to see Joe again. She avoided him at all costs. She was so afraid of what he was telling his friends about her. Missy was disgusted with herself, too, for letting things get out of hand. Why didn't she beat him up or slap him a good one? Missy realized that she didn't have the confidence and was afraid of rejection. She went to confession and bravely told her parents what had happened. She was careful to always keep away from the Octopus and others like him. Until she knew a guy, she decided it was best to only hang out with friends while in a group.

Missy was lucky that she got away from the Octopus with her virginity. Tracy wasn't so fortunate. Tracy was a lovely nineteen year old who went on a date with a guy she had known from high school. He was a couple of years older and was home from the service. They went to dinner and went dancing. The Octopus was taking her home when he pulled onto a deserted gravel road. Thinking things would be innocent enough, Tracy didn't object at first. That is until the Octopus kept forcing himself on her. Tracy begged and cried for him to stop but he refused. That night, in a car on a gravel road, the Octopus stole Tracy's virginity. She was so ashamed. The Octopus was shipped out overseas and Tracy was left to pick up the pieces. A few weeks later, Tracy discovered she was pregnant. What a nightmare! Unfortunately she made the choice, out of sheer panic, to abort the child. She realized later what a horrible mistake the abortion was and Tracy still carries this burden today. If only she had talked to her mother, things could have been different. This kind of stuff can happen when you're alone with the Octopus. Just be careful girls and be smart if you're alone with a guy. Feel free to do whatever you have to in order to get away. That means it's ok to hit, slap, kick, or spit. If you or anyone you know is ever in a situation like the above, don't keep it to yourself. Tell your parents and friends, and report the Octopus. He should have to take responsibility for his actions. This should make him ashamed, not the girl.

The Narcissist

The Narcissist is handsome, smooth and all the girls are crazy for him. He can be the football player or the musician. He comes in all varieties. In a nutshell though, he's all about himself. He dates the girls that will make him look good. Everything he does is for his benefit. He is a self-worshipper. If you go out with the Narcissist, it won't take long for you to realize that it's all about him. Girls who fall for this guy try to get his love but they never get it because he doesn't have any to give. The Narcissist spends all his time, energy and love on himself. There's really no story to tell because he never lasts in a relationship.

The Dreamer

The Dreamer is second cousin to the Bum. They have some of the same characteristics. The Dreamer has things he wants to do but somehow his dreams never materialize. He doesn't want a real job; he just chases a dream without putting the work into it that would actually make things happen. Lots of girls fall for the dreamer because he's creative, artistic and fun to be around. The Dreamer is a free spirit that doesn't follow convention.

Jenni met the Dreamer when she was in college. He was cute and interesting and had money from his parents. Craig had a motorcycle and liked to watch the stars at night. Jenni loved doing things with him. They would take hikes, rides on the motorcycle and watch the stars. Jenni never made her curfew when they were together. Her parents worried when she went out with Craig because they never knew what they were going to do or where they were going. Jenni was supposed to text her folks just to let them know where she was but she always forgot.

One night Jenni and Craig took off on his motorcycle to a park in a bad part of town. Of course they were oblivious to any danger. They spent the evening talking and having a midnight picnic under the stars. When Craig finally brought Jenni home, her father was up waiting and worrying. Jenni told her dad where they had been and apologized for forgetting to text or call to let him know where she was. Jenni's father freaked when she told him where they had gone.

Just two years before, her father had a friend whose daughter was murdered in the park where Jenni and Craig had been. The area was a hangout for a certain gang. The Dreamer never thinks about reality or what could happen because he has his head in the clouds. Craig was a Dreamer. Soon he left Jenni to traipse across Europe with a backpack and she never heard from him again.

The Brainiac

The Brainiac is your typical kind-of-nerdy guy. He's smart, likes school, has goals and ambitions and is an overall nice guy. Girls in high school and in college overlook him all the time. As time goes on, the Brainiac gets good grades, graduates with honors and lands a fantastic job. That's because he uses his brains to accomplish things in life. Smart girls realize the Brainiac is a good guy to get to know. They end up being the best husbands because they are goal oriented and are able to support a family.

Susie was in college and working at a restaurant when she met Paul. Susie's fellow waiters introduced the two over a game of darts one night. Susie was an outgoing and boisterous girl who liked having fun. Paul was quiet and studious. He was in Pharmacy school studying for his doctorate degree. The two were paired up to play darts and Susie started talking with Paul, whose quiet demeanor made having a conversation a bit difficult. But Susie liked Paul's quiet ways. After several meetings with friends and darts, Paul asked Susie for an official date. The two complemented each other's personalities and ended up getting married.

The Brainiac intimidates a lot of girls. Don't let smarts scare you. Everyone has gifts and being the Brainiac is a gift. You may be a female version of the Brainiac and that's awesome. Don't let the Brainiac get away if his brains intimidate you. Give him a chance and see what happens.

The Nice Guy

The Nice Guy is just that: nice. He is polite, kind, has goals and is just the all around good Joe. This is the kind of guy to look for in a husband. Unfortunately, a lot of girls find the Nice Guy to be dull, or think they don't deserve someone so nice. Too bad for them. The Nice Guy gets dumped by girls all the time and told, "You're just too nice." Those girls should have given the Nice Guy a chance because he's "what you see is what you get."

The Nice Guy is a gentleman and would never try things on a girl. He respects women and treats them well. He doesn't use bad language or tell dirty jokes around women. He goes to Church and loves his Mama. When he takes a girl out, he pays; he opens the door to let the women walk in first, he pulls the chair out for her and listens to her conversation. He uses good manners at dinner and asks if he can call you again if he likes her. If he doesn't want another date, he will thank the girl but he won't promise to call. Don't be too quick to dump the nice guy. Give him a chance. He may turn out to be a treasure. Whatever happens, you'll never have regrets for giving the Nice Guy a chance.

The Cheater

The Cheater likes to keep all his options open. He usually is a liar because he has to keep all the girls he is seeing in the dark about each other. The Cheater has an appeal that girls like, or else he wouldn't have more than one relationship going at a time. He will make you feel special and spend money on you to keep you around. The Cheater will tell you what you want to hear. He doesn't want commitment because he can't be with just one woman. He goes from relationship to relationship. Lots of girls let the Cheater get away with this behavior because they believe his lies or they don't have the confidence that they can do better. Make no mistake girls; you can always do better than the Cheater!

The Macho Man

The Macho Man has to have everything his way and he keeps a girl in her place – it's all about control. This is the kind of guy that can turn abusive because he has to have control. At first he is attentive and he makes the girl feel special. Slowly he cuts off all her friends and activities that don't include him. She isn't allowed to spend time with girlfriends or have any kind of life without him. This is the time to run like the wind girls. This is not good.

A 19-year-old girl named Julie found this all out the hard way. She started dating John in college and enjoyed his attentiveness. He called her often and liked knowing all the things she was doing. After a few months, Julie realized that she didn't really do anything without John and she had lost all her girlfriends. Now John was trying to get her to distrust her family. One day, Julie brought these things up to John. By now they were engaged. John went into a rage when Julie suggested that she should be able to see her friends and family whenever she wanted. He accused her of cheating on him and wanting to hurt him. He became so angry he locked her in his apartment bathroom and left for the entire day. After this incident, Julie found a way to get home to her parents and get rid of the Macho Man.

Ladies, if anyone tries to control who your friends are and what you do when they aren't around, it's a good sign that you are with a Macho Man. You need to get rid of him and find a Nice Guy or a Brainiac.

The Hard Worker

The Hard Worker is found in all walks of life. He's the farmer, the engineer, the plumber or teacher. Whatever he does, he does 100 percent. He's the guy that studies and worries about his grades and his social life may be nonexistent. He's the guy in high school who has his future mapped out to go on to college or to start a business. He has a high work ethic and is honest and true.

The Hard Worker is a good guy to date because he doesn't mess around with things that don't matter. If he's dating, there's a pretty good chance he's ready to find a wife and settle down. Don't date him unless you are ready for a commitment. If you are, he's a good find girls, so don't pass up the Hard Worker.

Did you know...

Many years ago, during the time of horses and carriages, the sign of a true gentleman was someone who made sure that he walked on the street side of the sidewalk while the lady walked on the inside? Can you figure out why? Well, it is because the horses would do their "business" as they walked by and sometimes their "business" would plop and splash people on the street. A gentleman would want to make sure that his lady wasn't splashed by mud or any other things that may have been making their way towards the pedestrians. Now that's the kind of man God wants for you, a daughter of the King, to have if you are called to the vocation of marriage!

Roman Hands and Russian Fingers

So, you decide that you want to date this guy. You don't know him very well, but he seems nice and you think he's cute. After a couple of times going to dinner or the movies, he has "Roman hands" and "Russian fingers." You know you are not ready for the intimacy he wants and you know it's wrong, but he's so cute and fun to be around. How are you supposed to handle this? Well, girlfriend the first thing you need to realize is that he's not the guy for you. If he is pushing you to do things you are uncomfortable with, he's selfish and thinking of his own desires. Not only that, but the two of you do not have the same morals. It is strongly suggested that he be dumped immediately. Let's say you want to give him a few more chances because you really like him. Well, you better have a conversation with him to explain what you expect from him and what kind of a girl you are. You're a nice girl and nice girls don't mess around! Most likely, he won't care so feel free to say, "Arrivederci!"

This all sounds so easy; but it's not, especially if you are attracted to a guy. Many girls cave in, when it comes to their morals, just to keep a guy around. Remember, you have value and dignity. You don't need a guy who makes physical demands on you. Save yourself a lot of grief and learn this now. Many, many young women give themselves away just to be ditched and left hurt and depressed. Keep your standards high ladies, and you'll see that it will be worth it.

So, what if you're the girl that is seen as the "buddy" to guys? This can feel bad especially if you really like one of the buddies. But, believe it or not, actually you are the lucky one. You see, you are learning more about guys and relationships than the girls that date one guy after another and give themselves away. For one thing you have your self-respect and that is priceless. Without knowing it, you are preparing yourself for the vocation of marriage by learning how to get along with guys in a nonphysical way. You don't have the baggage that immorality brings a girl.

Again, ladies, you have to remember the simple but profound purpose of your life to know, love and serve God in this life and to be happy with Him forever in the next. He has a plan for you. You will find the guy for you if marriage is your vocation.

Don't worry about dating because your Heavenly Father has taken care of all the details of your life. This isn't always easy to put into practice. Again, you will need your faith and your prayer life to lean on if you ever feel lonely in this area.

A physical relationship outside marriage is not only wrong and a serious sin, it is damaging to the people involved. God designed the marital act and the acts that lead up to it only for marriage because of the immense intimacy it provides. When two people engage in physical intimacy before marriage, they are operating not only in the physical realm but the spiritual as well.

The marriage act is symbolic of the oneness and the love of the Holy Trinity, Father, Son and Holy Spirit and for the love Christ has for His bride, the Church. Once you become one physically with someone, that bond cannot be broken, even if you break up with the person. It will always be a part of you. If you go on to marry another, there will be images in your mind that never go away of those that are not your spouse.

Many women experience deep depression after breaking off a physical relationship. There are those who turn to drugs and alcohol to ease the pain they feel after such a relationship. Even worse, if the woman does not go to confession, her relationship with God will also be broken. If you have fallen in this area, you can start over by going to confession and striving to live a pure life in the future. Anything can be forgiven!

Mary Magdalene is the saint who did just that. The Bible says she had seven demons driven from her and that she lived an impure lifestyle. Also remember the woman caught in adultery who was about to be stoned. Jesus reached out to her, ministered to her and forgave her.

He will do the same for anyone who wants to start over!

Real Love

Love is the giving of self. Many happily married couples will tell you it is complete self-sacrifice.

Here are a few examples:

✝ A husband is in an accident that leaves him unable to work and the wife cares for him and takes on a job so that their family will have a home and food.

✝ A young, newly married woman finds out she is pregnant. Soon she is very ill and has to stay in bed due to complications. Her husband takes over the household chores and lovingly takes care of her.

✝ A wife hates to cook and clean but does it cheerfully to please her husband.

✝ A husband is very frugal and thinks it's a waste of money to buy cards and small gifts for his wife but happily does it to please her.

Love is so much more than passion or romance. The words "I love you" are thrown around so casually today. Think before you say these precious words to someone. These words should only be said to a person that you are ready to marry. Of course you love your family and your friends and telling them you love them is perfectly fine. However when you say them to a guy, it should be special.

The examples above aren't romantic or exciting; in fact they are hard and mundane at times. But this is the stuff of true love. It is the stories we read in Scripture about Sarah and Abraham and the way in which St. Joseph loved the Blessed Mother.

Yes it's nice to feel butterflies in your stomach when your guy calls but these things fade as time goes on.

Commitment and a pledge of mutual fidelity and respect through an entire life together is the same kind of love that Christ has for you and why He wouldn't want you to settle for anything less.

John Paul II wrote a series of talks that are now called the "Theology of the Body." He wanted to teach people about how much God loves them. He explained that the marital union of married couples mirrored the love of the Trinity, as stated earlier. This human act brings two together and they become one in a beautiful and giving way. The pope believed this to be the most powerful way to show the love of the Trinity for each other and the love of God for us.

John Paul goes on to explain that the male and female body, in and of themselves, explains many things about man and woman that are unspoken. The man's body shows masculinity and he is called to be the giver of love, which is shown by the fact that his intimate parts are on the outside of his anatomy. He is the initiator of love and pursues the woman. This is not a cultural or learned behavior but something that is stamped in his very being, in his physical body.

Ladies, if you find yourself being the pursuer of men, think again. This type of behavior steals away the masculinity of a man. He may be flattered at first, but what you are really saying to a guy when you ask him out first or text him over and over, is that you don't think he's man enough to come after you. This is really an insult. Granted, some guys need to take more initiative to begin relationships. However, ladies, give them a break here. Since the feminist movement (we'll discuss it in detail later in the book), men have become confused on how to act around women. It's up to you to help teach guys how to be gentlemen and initiate relationships – which are nonphysical but filled with kindness and caring. Women are smart, creative and intuitive. There are plenty of ways to get a guy to pursue you without taking over or being manipulative. When a man pursues the woman, he is honoring her. When a woman pursues, she is desperate and insecure.

The woman, too, has meaning. It is apparent in the way she has been created. Her intimate parts are veiled, hidden within her anatomy. She is the receiver of love. In the Song of Solomon, a beautiful garden is used to describe woman.

You are the keeper of your "secret garden" and only you allow entrance by your invitation and the only one who should be allowed to enter is your husband, for he is the only one worthy. When a woman wears suggestive clothing she is giving the message to men that she will give herself to him and to anyone who will give her attention. Modesty, veiling what should remain hidden, will reveal to a man the woman's dignity. He will see how she sees herself. Women dream of being pursued by a worthy man.

God has a plan for every young woman's life. Let Him bring *you* a worthy suitor. Trust that if you are being called to the vocation of marriage, God will provide you with a worthy and suitable husband as long as you do your part, which is to uphold your own dignity and value.

Remember you are worth more that a precious jewel and are unique. It's never, never, never acceptable to act desperate, and that includes you being the "pursuer." By allowing a gentleman to make an effort to pursue you, you will make him want you more. You've got to put a little mystery in things and should not make yourself so available that there is no secrecy about you to others. When your parents feel you are ready to date, don't be available every time you are asked out. Don't be so quick to answer his texts, calls or emails. Let him wonder a little what you're doing. It's never okay to settle.

Years ago, women expected men to treat them with respect. Women celebrated their true femininity by letting men take care of them by displaying behaviors such as opening the car door, pushing in their chair, paying for their meal, letting them go first, and so on.

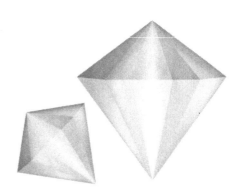

A gentleman is a man of good, courteous conduct. Nowadays, being a gentleman has not been a priority for many men. When the feminist movement started, things changed for the worse. Many women decided that they did not need a man to take care of them. They could take care of themselves. This is true in many cases: women are educated, have careers and can support themselves in a way unheard of in past times. But now, some women feel offended when a man opens a door for them. This is ridiculous!

As a woman, expect to be treated with the dignity that God has given every woman. Appreciate these small gestures of respect. A true gentleman displays basic good manners.

Is he a true gentleman?

✞ Is courteous to all people, even those he dislikes

✞ Keeps his cool at all times

✞ Dresses appropriately for the occasion

✞ Owns at least one pair of dress shoes

✞ Holds the door open for you

✞ Has good table manners

✞ Is able to carry a conversation with people of all ages

✞ Shows concern when someone is hurting

✞ Offers to help you carry a heavy package

✞ Takes care of his appearance and personal hygiene

✞ Takes his cap off at the table

✞ Opens and closes car doors for women

✞ Stands and offers his chair to a woman in a crowded place when there are none available

✞ Allows the woman to order her dinner first or asks her what she wants and orders for her

Or is he a slob in the making?

✞ Spits in public

✞ Sneezes and coughs without covering his mouth

✞ Interrupts you when you are talking

✞ Belches and farts loudly and doesn't excuse himself

✞ Pressures you into doing something you don't want to do

✞ Swears

✞ Leaves the toilet a mess and doesn't put the seat down

✞ Has zero table manners

✞ Expects you to pay for his meal when you go out

✞ Doesn't take care of his personal hygiene

✞ Wears a cap at the table

✞ Licks his knife

✞ Doesn't pick up a woman at her home but expects her to drive

✞ Honks and expects her to run out to the car if he does drive

So, how did he stack up?

If you see a lot of the "slob" characteristics, you've got some work to do in educating the guys in your life on gentlemanly behavior.

Do you know Marie and Shawn?

Marie and Shawn had been dating for months and were talking about marriage. Marie really loved Shawn and appreciated his attentive, gentle, and sincere personality. However, from the beginning of their relationship, she could see that Shawn had developed some bad habits in college while living with a bunch of guys. He licked his fingers and even his plate sometimes. He reached over people to grab the food he wanted, talked with his mouth full, used his fork like a shovel, always had his elbows on the table, and interrupted others in conversation. Although these things seem trivial, they really bugged Marie.

As time went on, she found ways of gently telling Shawn of his bad manners. Once they were engaged, she figured she could be a little more blunt. So, one evening as the two had dinner together, Marie kindly said to Shawn, "You know Shawn, soon you will be graduating with your advanced degree. You'll be a professional out there in the working environment. You may want to appear more polished, you know, not like a 'frat rat." He was receptive to her so she continued. "You've developed some rather nasty table manners and I want to help you improve on them so you won't embarrass yourself when you have to entertain clients or go on interviews. Would you mind that?" Shawn agreed that he did behave like a slob at times and was open to Marie when she gave him little hints and corrections. Marie and Shawn have been married now for fifteen years. There are still times she gives him gentle reminders about his table manners but all in all, he's not a slob any more.

Here are some suggestions on how to help the men in your life (brothers, cousins, neighbors and friends) become gentlemen. Remember, though, not to nag or complain or you won't like the results.

- Do not go out to the car if the guy honks his car horn. If he calls on his cell phone and wonders why you're not coming out, tell him, "You need to come in when you pick me up."
- Don't get out of the car unless the guy comes around to open and close the door for you. If he wonders why you are not getting out, this is the perfect opportunity to let him know what you expect of him. Just say, "It is good manners for you to open and close the door for me."
- If you are walking in your high heels and the guy is a block ahead of you, call out to him," Hey! I'm back here!"
- If he goes through the door first, stand and wait for him to open it for you. Again, if he wonders why you're not opening it yourself, say, "It's good manners for you to open the door and let me walk in first."
- If you go to Church with a guy and he wears a baseball cap but doesn't remove it, say, "You should take your hat off in Church."
- If you go to a nice place to eat, and the guy doesn't hold your chair for you, don't sit down. Say, "It's good manners for you to get the chair for me."

These are the most basic of all manners a guy should know. This society has gotten so relaxed that many guys don't know them and girls don't expect them. If you don't expect it ladies, then you won't get it.

Remember you deserve to be treated like royalty because you in fact are; your Daddy's the King of the Universe!

Real, True Love

When it was time for Abraham's son, Isaac, to get married, Abraham did what any father would do. He sent his servant to find a wife for Isaac.

"What?!" You may be asking about now. "What do you mean 'sent his servant to find Isaac a wife?'"

After all, you'd be mortified if your parents picked your husband, right? You can't even trust your parents to pick your jeans, huh?

Well, maybe you would be freaked out and maybe you wouldn't. But let me ask you this: do you believe that your parents love and care about you and your future? Do you believe your parents have your best interests in mind? Come on. You can admit it, they aren't in the room. Parents always want the best for their children – even parents who don't do such a great "parenting" job.

Well, back in the day, marriages used to happen through arrangements. And, just so you know, marriages lasted a whole lot longer than they do now. People have forgotten how important things like faith and parent involvement and mutual backgrounds are in building a good marriage.

But let's get back to the story...

So Abraham, quite old by now, sends his servant to find a wife for Isaac. Abraham makes his servant give an oath that he will go to Abraham's homeland and find the wife – none of the locals will do because they are idol-worshippers and Abraham realizes how important the wife's faith will be in her marriage to his beloved son and in raising the children.

So the servant takes the oath and sets off to find Isaac's wife. On the way the servant prays to God for some help. The servant has already been told by

Abraham that if the girl is not willing to come back to Isaac, then the servant is free from the oath.

This whole thing may seem a bit archaic to us but it is good to know that a woman would not be taken against her will to be a wife, right?

The servant knows that Isaac is a great, kind, and caring man who is close to his parents and is longing for a wife so that he can begin his own family. Taking this responsibility of finding a wife very seriously, the servant prays to God for some sort of sign so that the woman God has chosen for Isaac will be made known to the servant. Abraham wants her to be from his homeland and willing to move to Canaan while the servant wants even more. He asks God to show him the right woman by having her offer him water for his camels. That would be a kind thing to do and the servant knows that kindness is a beautiful characteristic in a wife. He wants that for Isaac.

Sure enough, the servant arrives at the town well of Abraham's homeland just in time for the arrival of the town's women who are fetching water for their homes and the needs of their family. The servant spots a beautiful woman and asks her for water. She replies, just as the servant had asked of God, with an offer to also give him water for the camels.

The servant is shocked and amazed! God had answered his prayers so clearly. The servant explains who he is and asks the woman, Rebekah, if she would like to come to Canaan and marry Isaac. She accepts this wonderful marriage offer and packs up and leaves with the servant for the journey.

The servant rode first on his camel and Rebekah followed on hers. Behind them would have been Rebekah's servant and the other camels with Rebekah's belongings.

When the journey ends and Rebekah and the servant arrive at Abraham's land it is sunset. Isaac is off in the distance and looms large and mysterious. Rebekah veils her face to maintain her modesty. Her heart is pounding at the prospect of meeting her future husband. The servant quietly goes off towards the house while Rebekah slips off the camel and looks at Isaac.

Their eyes meet and Isaac knows that this woman is the love of his life.

Modesty was a beautifully valued trait and because men and women understood that temptation towards acts or thoughts were easily instigated, the servant had Rebekah, riding on her camel, follow him versus the other way around. Think about it. What the servant knew was that if he followed Rebekah and watched her throughout the journey, his mind might wander to impure thoughts and to keep that from happening, he led the way.

Chastity and purity were also valued because they said a lot about a person's character. Someone who made the decision to stay chaste and pure was someone who could commit to other things in life – especially married life – which was an important trait because, well, marriage has lots of ups and downs. Someone who makes a commitment to chastity and purity is able to better handle the ups and downs of a marriage versus someone who gives in to temptations and self-gratifying behavior.

So here we have gorgeous Rebekah – because she was beautiful, Scripture says so – who was also modest and chaste and pure and kind. Isaac was going to be a lucky man!

Love a good love story?
The Story of Peace by Miriam Ezeh
is all about true love and right relationships.

Duct Tape Handbag

Materials Needed:

Scissors; Paper; Colored Duct Tape; Utility Knife

1. Choose one or more colors of duct tape for your bag
2. On paper, draw and cut out the pattern for your bag including, sides, bottom, and handle.
3. Lay out pattern pieces of the handbag.
4. Carefully, cut pieces of duct tape to the length of the pattern pieces.
5. Lay the tape on the paper and press firmly, careful not to make wrinkles.
6. Add the next piece of tape overlapping ¼ inch.
7. Continue until the paper is covered and you have done all the pieces of the pattern.
8. Using the tape, attach the pieces together, making sure to make a smooth edge.
9. You can use a utility knife to cut out designs to decorate your bag. Suggestions would be a flower, a checkered pattern, or polka dots.
10. Be creative and have fun!

Make a Difference in the World!

Lots of girls your age begin to feel a real call to "make a difference" in the world. There are loads of ways to do this. Consider some of the following while you pray and ask God for direction:

✝ Check in with your diocesan office or local parish center to see who needs what -- they will know if there is a person who needs meals or a family who needs help with the kids – ask your mom or dad to help you arrange your time so that you can offer your services to a person or family in need.

✝ Consider starting an "All Things Girl" tween group using the ATG Leader's Guide – you'll help young Catholic girls learn their true identity as daughters of the King – check out www.ATGSeries.com for books and supplies. Be a leader for Christ!

✝ Get a few friends together, have a garage sale and donate the proceeds to a local Catholic pro-life group.

Learning
from All
of God's
Creatures

Of Dead Squirrels

It is bound to happen. When you take four dogs for a walk in untenanted fields they are going to catch something once in awhile. One warm winter morning (I can say this in Alabama) my littlest rapacious hunter, Skye came home with a squirrel. I averted my gaze. Through her stuffed mouth she was growling the others away. She well knew they would have it off her in a heart beat.

For Skye, I am not sure it was such a wonderful gift. She had to guard it constantly. Because my pack follows me everywhere she could not lie down and enjoy her catch but had to carry it all over the place. Her growling and scowling continued unabated as she warned them away. She is the littlest and so must defend her own with the support of mama (me). That day she not only didn't enjoy her prize but missed out on the afternoon biscuit time — her mouth was full and she couldn't leave the poor thing for a moment. Pretty soon the squirrel was tattered beyond recognition.

It became clear to me as I did my farm chores that my pride was a lot like that dead squirrel. I am so invested in my self-love that I keep my teeth closed tightly on its rights and dignities. And because I cling so tightly to myself I am not available for God's wisdom and transformation. My growls as I defend myself drown out Our Lord's gentle, inexorable voice calling me to repentance and change.

God is about transforming me. He is about turning me around from my concupiscence into a holy life. His ways are not my ways. I am interested in clutching the dead squirrel of my opinions and values until it deprives me of life in the body of Christ. As Skye was appreciably exiled from the community of the pack by her prize — so am I when I judge others, shun others, or let my own self interest interfere with the business of serving Our Lord and my neighbor.

Who's in Charge?

It is common knowledge that if a horse has a problem, whether it be annoying, benevolent or just plain dangerous, it is the human's fault. There is no exception to this rule. As Marygate unfolds, I have realized that this is the rule for all the animals under my care. I must make an effort to be clearheaded more than "compassionate," farsighted more than circumstance driven and focused more than feeling.

My working dog, Hannah, is a case in point. Since all my other dogs are gratuitous boarders, I hadn't any experience of a real working animal. She is an
Anatolian Shepherd who has been trained to guard, guide and nurture goats. In my "compassionate" ignorance, I detected that she would much rather play with my other four dogs.

Soon, my goat helpmate was severely compromised! She didn't want to stay with the herd anymore. I felt sorry for her so I would let her out to play. Hannah is no different than anyone who is being offered a free ride and took to her new life of leisure with gusto. Command decisions had to be made or anarchy would be the order of the day. I gave Hannah mixed messages about what was required of her and compromised her work ethic.

Then there was the rotten decision of feeding one of my older orphan goats through the gate for convenience. Well, I felt sorry for the pregnant ones who wanted a midday snack too. I've been pregnant – I surely knew how they felt! So I began to feed them some treats. It didn't take long for them to destroy the wired netting that keeps babies from escaping through the gate. Plus, there is no love lost between goat mamas when there is food. Major skirmishes ensued while I tried to feed the baby kid its bottle. I had "trained" them through compassion to destroy the gate and each other!

As I have learned to gain mastery and wisdom over my animals – out of order and love – it became apparent to me that I could carry that into my spiritual life. It is a different form of self- mastery than I formerly practiced. My idea of self-denial and discipline was beating myself up mentally, downgrading myself, and setting impossible goals. I wouldn't even treat my animals this way so why was I treating a daughter of God likewise?

Our Lord has shown me how to be focused, fair, cool headed and loving as I strive for self-mastery. As I form and shape my animal's lives into order and happiness, so can I use those same gifts in my personal life as well.

My imagination has always been a gift – but she is a ship without a rudder many times. Her favorite pastime is worry – she is exponentially great at creating disastrous scenarios out of everyday life. When I feed my imagination with these treats only chaos and misery ensue.

For instance, when I ride my horse Sam out in the fields, if I see a cow a quarter of a mile away, it takes two seconds for me to have my horse turn tail and run, I fall off, get my foot caught in the stirrup and break my neck. Sam is afraid of cows and we are working on that – but I have to master my imagination and fear first. As you can infer, I don't have too many pleasant rides if I let my imagination run this way. And it occurred to me that my imagination is very well trained to the negative!

If my husband is late getting home it takes my imagination about two seconds to have him in a car wreck. No, my imagination is not a pretty thing. But what have I been feeding it? Like my goats – treats at inappropriate times and places. Like my dog Hannah I give it mixed messages. I beat it up when I know I am being anxious – yet feed it all kinds of anxious sweets.

Self-Mastery! Ah, what a beautiful, majestic word that gives us respect and wisdom for ourselves. I thank God that He has taken my passion for animals to grasp how I can grow in my wisdom and knowledge of Him. Self-respect has never come naturally to me, but as I learn to treat my animals with the respect that makes their lives happy I am glad to know I can turn that focus on my own life as well.

Stumped

It was a daunting task. It was the middle of July, the middle of the day under the achingly hot Alabama sun that we began. With a machete and loppers we had to clear a tick infested, thorn festooned fence line. The undergrowth was so horrendous that a bulldozer could not get through. Foot by painful foot we hacked away at every thorn ever created. It started me thinking about sin – probably because of St. Paul's words, "the sin that clings so closely." In the course of a few hours every patch of exposed skin was bleeding.

After this experience, and many other fence lines later, I began to see a pattern that helped me clear things a lot faster. Usually you have a stump. The tree either was cut down or fell. In its wake you get saplings and scrub brush. Vines that tangle the whole mess into impossible soup soon follow. In our case that particularly tedious day, the entanglement had been thirty years in the making. I found that if I located the stump and cleared the scrub I was removing the props that held the mass in place. It is still a painful, arduous task, but it goes much faster.

I realized that tackling sin could be done much the same way. As I pinpoint the "everyday sin" I pray for the Holy

Spirit to show me what the props to that sin might be. Then I go back even further to see where the rupture occurred. I call it the "clearing field" that begins the whole process. When I get to the stump – God can show me truly how to get rid of the whole mass.

It came together one of the times I went to confession. I was bothered by the fact (as was God, I am sure) that I repeatedly spoke poorly of a close relative. As I told the priest about it, I also confessed that I thought anger had a lot to do with this sin. He looked at me straight in the eye and said, "Let's step back a bit. I think that forgiveness is the issue, don't you?"

It was so illuminating that I was speechless. But I realized he was exactly right. And as I did my penance I took time to locate the stump. In the past a decision the relative had made hurt me and made me feel very disrespected. From that time I let hurt pride keep me from loving and trusting that person. Lack of forgiveness and anger were the props of my language and failure to conquer that particular sin. God had given me the tools to see into myself and to surrender my pride and hurt and truly forgive this person. But in the process I received something even better. I realized that in the incident God had given me an opportunity to suffer as His son suffered for all of our sins. If I had opened my arms in understanding and forgiveness to begin with all the tangled mass in the ensuing years need not have happened.

I never thought I would be thankful for "brother weeds" and "sister thorns" but it is good to know that those hours of hacking away not only cleared some fence lines but cleared a path to holiness as well.

The Pecking Order

Sam wanted the salt lick in a terrible way. He kept edging his nose toward the bucket, hoping against hope the mare would allow a few licks. Duchess, the mare, adroitly swung her haunches around, and with a squeal let her hind legs send Sam about his business. And what was that business? Actually, the story of Sam's life: waiting. Still, he began the hoof by hoof journey again and edged closer to the salt lick, hoping against hope.....

The pecking order amongst prey animals does not deviate. There is an established, immutable line up from the dominant to the docile. It isn't a democracy by all means. The strong minded rule the weak. By the same token, however, the meekest try every moment of their lives to get the first bite, the best pasture, the nicest shelter. They never quit trying to test the one in charge, looking for weakness.

As caretaker I must respect this pecking order. It is what they understand and what they expect. Even though I get a little frustrated at the downright meanness of the mare, or just meanness in general, it is important for me to allow the scene to play out.

Sam inches forward once again. Then Max finishes his breakfast and sends the mare about her business despite her flashing hind legs and angry squeals. Sam quits trying and knows he won't get the treat for a good while yet!

As I reflected upon the pecking order, I realized that Our Lord has a message of comfort in it for me. As the middle child and the only left handed one in my family, you can imagine how I felt lost in the shuffle. I had high-achieving, strong, older siblings and I seemed destined to bask only in the shadows. It wasn't until I was in my forties that I realized that I wasn't stupid and inept.

Because of my left handedness, I did (and do) everything backwards until I unscramble it in my brain.

A wonderful karate teacher taught me to be patient with myself. Once I realized that the task wasn't impossible, but that I must "learn" it in a different way, lots of things in my life began to make sense.

I remember when I was ten years old, I was standing in a field and I promised God that one day I would be famous. I wanted my name to be made known – I wanted to accomplish great things! This, even though I had trouble coloring in the lines! Older and wiser now, I still fall into the trap of trying to do "one great thing" for God. It is an insecurity device for I have learned that the only thing I need to do is what God wants me to do.

So what in the world does that have to do with the pecking order? It is this: I have my place in the body of Christ. I have my tasks that the Lord gives me every day. I don't need to lead the herd or wish I was someone I am not. God does destine certain people for greatness; their personalities lead us, inspire us and pull us along in their wake. As I watched the great film *Amazing Grace,* it comforted me to know that God has a plan for each human person. I don't have to be a William Wilberforce and go down in the annals of history for the abolition of slavery. But I can quietly do my little part to end abortion, comfort the sick, feed the hungry and proclaim the truth. I might be somewhere indeterminate in the pecking order of the human race as far as gifts and abilities go – but there is only one thing needed: to do the Will of the One who created me. This is exactly what the most sublime Person ever did: what His Father willed.

As the Worm Turns

Suffice it to say that when you have animals you have to deal with worms. Most pet owners know this and give their little darling a nice chewable pill once a month and everyone is happy. As you get into the larger species and their different worm loads the scheduling and doses become a nightmare.

However, it is something that is so vital to the health of your livestock, I must monitor what and when as well as evaluating the wormer's effectiveness. Worming, as you can imagine, has taught me quite a bit about my spiritual life.

In keeping with the American way – that is marketing – there are all kinds of wormers on the shelf. There are daily wormers, weekly wormers, monthly wormers so that the problem can be dealt with as palatably as possible. There are apple and peppermint flavors, easy injectors – you name it. Then there is the data on worm medicine. If there are three experts, there are at least four opinions, statistics included.

When you have horses, goats, dogs and cats you have to deal with time frame and doses. Some are once a month, some are every other month, some are every twelve weeks and then the whole thing changes according to their behavior and the conjunctiva of the eye! This worming in cycles has taught me to "know myself" so that I can be ready for the bad mood, the stressful reaction and the situations conducive to sinful behavior. I am not very good at it yet, (ask my husband) but I am able to anticipate stepping outside God's grace.

Maybe it seems odd to say but worming my animals is a constant reminder to me to evaluate my spiritual life. Half of controlling worms is environment. Keeping the living areas clean and the water troughs sparkling is one way. I ask myself, what is the make up of my environment? Do I watch five times more television that reading scripture? What is the first thing I do in the morning and the last thing I do at night? So, as I adjust my spiritual reading and study, I am halfway there: I effectively eliminate the environment conducive to sinful behavior and thought. As Jesus said that it was what came out of a person that defiled so I strive to keep the innards clean and well read.

One great way to keep your livestock healthy from invaders is good feed, clean water and supplements as needed. If they have fresh air and plenty of roaming space, your animals have a much easier time fighting off parasites.

It reminds me of the Scripture, Matthew 12:43-45. In it Jesus tells of a man whose unclean spirit was cast out of him. But finding no other dwelling place, the demon returns and finds the man's interior swept *but empty*. So the devil goes and gets seven others and the man is in worse state than before. It isn't enough to get rid of sin and bad habits. I must allow the Lord power over my interior life to keep me safe from evil. I must be proactive to keep my spiritual channels open to the grace of the Holy Spirit and my will especially pliant to His Will.

One very important fact regarding worming is record keeping. I simply cannot trust my memory amongst so many different needs. If I don't write it down right away, heaven help me! No longer can I juggle these things in my head. It has helped me to schedule and commit to a regular celebration of the Sacrament of Confession. No longer do I want to go before the priest and stutter, "It has been – I don't know – how long since my last confession." By committing to a regular time I am declaring that the sacrament is vital to my spiritual health; and the Lord can meet me there with the correct "wormer" for my soul's needs.

The Sacrament of Reconciliation

is the best wormer on the market!

Happy Tails

As you can imagine, I am covered up in tails. I have amongst my animals, dog tails, goat tails, cat tails, chicken tails and donkey tails. Some wag when they see me coming. Some wag as they eat. Some are feathers that blow in the breeze. Very  often I wonder what it would be like if God gave us tails and how would we use them? I read a short story about the idea years ago. Then it occurred to me that we do have tails of a sort.

It never ceases to amaze me that my dogs display the utmost delight in everything I do. When they haven't seen me for five minutes or five hours, there goes the waving tail.

While pondering this phenomenon, the realization of human "tails" made me smile. Okay so it is the other end! However, we can change so much within ourselves and a situation by a simple smile. It is as easy as wafting a tail. Or is it?

There is a movie that talks about happiness. In it, there are thirteen people whose lives are connected and are unaware that their fates are connected also. The critical point of the whole movie is seen in the simple expression of a smile. This seemingly small gesture prevents a young girl from killing herself. A man's single smile lights in her a will to live; a will to not submit to futility.

I am always surprised that my dogs wag their tails whenever they see me. Their tail wagging is as unconditional as the God's love to all of humanity.

I realized that my smile is as necessary and free to all who cross my path. The simple smile changes my attitude; it shows interest and respect. I am amazed at how the smile changes the complexion of every human transaction I undertake.

And, as I smile, it makes the inside of me smile also. Cost what it may, the smile is mine to give – to wag as it were – and change the face of every situation and every relationship. Sounds simple doesn't it? Although I hope to never see fur on my lips, I hope that God can use my smile as one of His great gifts to me. And, I sincerely hope that every time I see one of my five dog's tails wag, it can remind me to be loving and kind to all.

There is a story I used to read to my children and recall it often. It is entitled, "What Is the Worth of a Smile?" It is a true story of a little girl who smiled at an elderly gentleman and made him feel welcome. That man left her a hundred thousand dollars in his will! I am not looking for those kinds of riches but the point is clear: that smile made that man feel like a million dollars. It gave him hope. It made him feel like a human person. How can I help all who cross my path to feel like a child of God?

Dwight and Old Wood

Dwight was sitting on an old stump carefully watching a hole in the ground. He had dug many such holes, poured water into them and now the wait began. It was a sticky hot Alabama day and the shade from the forest was blessed. As I waited with him, I tried to find out more about this interesting man. He had worked in forestry for many years and, now retired; he perked land for prospective builders such as me.

My land was not cooperating. The water stubbornly stayed in the hole much past the required time limits. So, we decided to work our way back into the woods. As we walked, I described our lofty plan to clean up the wooded area on our land. Loggers had previously cut – years ago – the large timber consequently leaving unprotected saplings. As they grew to adulthood, the saplings looked very much like "Dr Seuss" trees. Stumps, old branches and countless bits of dead wood fostered vines and scrub. It wasn't attractive.

He looked at me in his quiet way, sizing me up I suppose, and said, "Don't clean it all up like that. Leave it for small animals – they need a home and protection."

Years later I am glad that I took his advice. Rabbits and squirrels abound. My goats love jumping on all the old piles of tree trunks. How boring the landscape would be if I had reduced it to a park land! And what a dangerous place for my wooded friends to live in!

As I learn about the Sacrament of Reconciliation, Dwight's advice comes to the foreground. If I had my way, I would have bulldozed the old wood right out of my life in one compelling sweep. Our Lord, in His wisdom, is teaching me that preserving the piles is what redemption is all about. Instead of wiping out my sins and shortcomings, He redeems them so that they may be of use to someone else. Or, bring me closer to Him.

For instance, I have become very aware lately of two things. One, God wants to work on some very difficult things in my past that affect my present. Two, confession is the way it will be healed. Okay, Lord, bring in the bulldozer! Let's get this out once and for all! I want my sin gone as much as anybody but He, in His love and mercy, knows I can't take it. So the piles remain as He one-by-one transforms them into life. The pile left might be wisdom for someone else in the future. It might be a steady reminder of His goodness and forbearance. The landscape of my life must be crafted and healed and transformed – not eradicated.

One interesting thing I have learned is that celebrating the Sacrament often allows God to use it more effectively in my life and to expose more of what He wants to forgive and transform. It has taken me a long time to learn this: God's ways of grace are not my natural paths. The more I surrender to Him, intersect with Him through the Sacraments, the better able I am to get rid of the "laundry list" and let Him reveal my sins. Confession has become one of the most powerful, provocative and life-changing graces in my life. And at the bottom of it is this: His mercy endures forever!

Now I have fashioned paths in my woods. I have dug gardens and planted. I have created some "park land." But I think I have the greatest appreciation for my piles of old wood. These piles teem with life as my own "piles" teem with transformation. Thanks, Dwight, for your wonderful insight!

Loving Them Across

My friend Joanne accosted me as I walked into her barn. She was spattered with mud all the way to her eyebrows. I had seen that look before and it had been on my own face.

"I've been trying to get Lily across the ditch for the last three hours," she gasped, "Will you help me?"

At the back of her property was a very luscious ravine at the bottom of which was a creek bed. Months before, my horse Max and I had a major altercation over this same ditch.

To me, the creek wasn't anything scary at all. To Max it was the Grand Canyon. So Joanne and I took her young filly down the ravine. She explained that she had tried for hours to get the horse to jump over the ditch but was unsuccessful. Judging by Lily's rolling eyes and tense, twitching muscles, it was going to be difficult. But I had remembered my lessons with Max very well.

"Look," I proposed, "Let's do it a different way."

"What do you mean?" she asked.

I smiled and said, "Let's love her across."

"What?"

"I've been through this with Max," I explained, "Lily doesn't trust us. Let's be very calm. We have to accept that she might not cross today....but if we work on it with love, she will someday."

Joanne, fortunately, was open to learning. "Okay," she said, "Show me what you mean."

Using my natural horsemanship training, I began to stroke Lily and urged her to calm down and not get so excited about the ditch. We focused on confidence and authority. In fifteen minutes we had her across. In twenty she went back and forth with no worries. I learned so much from those experiences.

You can't spout formulas or Scripture verses to most people. You can't introduce them to a loving God unless you do what Jesus did: *love them across.* For so many people, life has splattered them all over the pavement. A ditch is a chasm – truly an abyss separating them from all happiness. They can't get there by words alone, deeds are critical, loving deeds that give them the confidence to ask just the simplest question: Do you love me Jesus? Until they get to that point, all they see is the unsurpassable ditch.

I have learned from my horses that no tiny deed goes unnoticed. Every stroke, every word builds a relationship of trust. It cannot be rushed and it must be maintained.

How much more should I be prepared to love those whom I find across that great divide? Every little deed, service or word must add to the crossing of that bridge. If I focus on loving my fellow beings across the abyss to God's love, then I have been able to accomplish the miraculous things Jesus promised.

Keeping in Line

In the early days of my newfound horse passion, I read lots "how to" books. After being overwhelmed by one such tome I grasped the easiest thing I could handle. The author said, "If you cannot ride a horse in a straight line then you are not a good rider." Eagerly I saddled Max and went out to earn my spurs.

A few hours later I realized that it is **impossible** to ride a horse in a straight line. Frustrated and angry I got off because I knew it wasn't Max's fault – he just couldn't go straight! In the months to come I  never did master the straight line and it haunted me.

Years later, once I embarked on natural horsemanship, I again confronted the straight line. Come on! I had put that behind me! However it would prove to be one of the most valuable lessons I have ever learned from God. Thankfully, this course taught you how to do it. Now with valuable training I was ready to master the straight line!

I had to master myself first. Focus was essential. Lots and lots of riders have the bad habit of looking down when riding. I think particularly people who school horses. It is also a habit of riders who aren't very secure. I speak from personal history. I had to break the habit of looking down. After all you wouldn't drive a car that way! I had to learn to focus on an object in the distance and send my horse there. It wasn't about the line, but about the goal. I had to keep myself balanced and straight to my goal. It would, in time, direct the horse.

Then I had to pull a little on the reins when Max would veer out of line. I would say, for about a hundred feet of line, I had to give Max about fifty corrections. It wasn't discipline exactly but training Max to listen to my focus and to help him learn the straight line.

It didn't take long for Our Lord to transpose this lesson into my spiritual life. I realized that going straight wasn't my strong point. In order to conquer sinful habits, untrusting attitudes and unloving actions I had to focus. I had to stop looking at my failures in these areas and get my eyes up and looking at Christ. He is the goal. When I focus on my failures I can't walk straight, let alone see straight. It takes trusting Him to let go of my familiar burdens. I have to believe the truth: He has set me free from them.

Balancing my spiritual self consists of Scripture, Church teaching, sacraments, daily service (not in that order) and of course, prayer. These must be in balance if I am to ride straight to my goal.

As remorse, regret and repentance surface, it is so easy for me to hate myself. God does not shine the light on my sins to condemn me – but to free me. Once I was able to focus on the truth: God hates my sin, but loves me, I was able to see the goal. Just as Max required endless patience and tiny corrections, I learned to give myself the same latitude.

Max and I ride a straight line just by looking at the goal now. He is in tune with my focus. Focus, balance and endless corrections (speaking truth) have kept me in line – onward towards Christ.

A Picture Collage Is Fun To Do!

If you have lots of pictures that are tucked away in albums and you'd like to do something fun and exciting with them, consider making a picture collage. Picture collages are fairly easy and fun to make.

Here's what you need and what you will do:

Gather your old pictures that are tucked away in albums or sitting in shoe boxes. Make sure you only grab pictures that you know will be okay to be cut and pasted.

Once you have all your pictures, lay them out on the floor or a table to see what size frame you will need. Some people have huge family picture collages hanging in their foyer while others have a small picture collage on their desks or dressers.

Begin cutting out the pictures so that the main thing you have is the head and/or a bit of a body or background. In some cases you'll want more than in others. For instance, if the picture is from a birthday party and you are blowing out the cake – include the cake! This can be a painstaking process so give yourself a few days to accomplish this so your work doesn't get sloppy.

Once all your pictures are cut out, use a thick cardboard for a back on which to glue each picture. The cardboard should fit nicely within the frame so check that out before you begin! Once you know the cardboard works well in the frame, place your pictures on it to get a sense of how they can be arranged. Sometimes a backing on the cardboard works nice – especially if you anticipate a bit of empty spaces between the pictures.

When you have an idea of the placement of your pictures you can begin lifting each one individually and dabbing it with a glue stick – not too much glue because you don't want the picture bumpy.

The best picture collages have no white space showing between the pictures so if you didn't put a backing (like a pretty scrap of wallpaper piece or fabric remnant) you can use additional pictures to fill in; or, you can get creative and use anything else that will personalize your picture collage.

More Crafts...

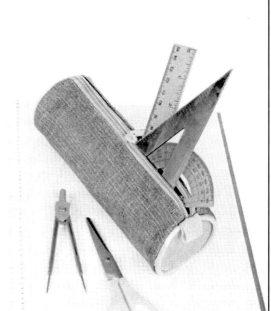

Tissue Paper Decoupage Shoes

Materials Needed: 1 pair of Canvas Shoes; Colored tissue paper; Outdoor Mod Podge; Medium sized paintbrush

Directions
1. Choose 1-3 colors of tissue
2. Tear into 1-inch pieces
3. Using the paintbrush beginning at the toe, brush on the Mod Podge
4. Lay the pieces of tissue at the toe along the curve, tearing the pieces to fit
5. Overlap the edges to create pretty combinations of color.
6. When the tissue covers the entire shoe, brush on a topcoat of Mod Podge
7. Use several coats of topcoat for durability
8. Buy fancy shoestrings to match or add pony beads for creativity

Make your own Body Glitter

Materials Needed: Clear Aloe Vera gel; Fine Colored glitter; Small container

Directions
1. Fill your container ¾ of the way with Aloe Vera gel
2. Sprinkle a little glitter at a time and stir well
3. Add as much glitter as you like
4. Rub on arms, and neck for a sparkling accessory

Thank you

When is the last time you wrote a "Thank you" note? Has it been awhile? How about a letter to a friend who has moved away or to a relative you haven't seen in awhile?

You may be like many teens today and your favorite mode of communication is texting or emails. But there is nothing like a real, honest-to-goodness handwritten note to make someone's day! So go ahead – pick up a pen and a pretty sheet of paper and write a note of love, gratitude or just to say "hello!" You'll be glad you did.

Thinking of you!

I hope you are doing well in your new school!

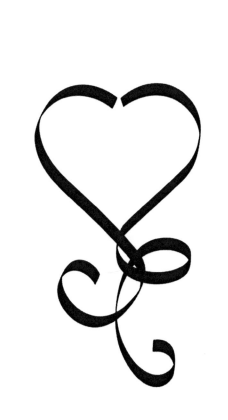

Influences
from the
Feminist
Movement

Maybe some of the things addressed in this book seem old-fashioned and out of touch to you. Maybe part of you squirms at the idea of a genteel manner in which the man opens the door or changes the flat tire on a car. Or maybe you know a few friends who bristle at the idea of motherhood and homemaking. Sadly, much of that type of attitude can be attributed to the feminist movement of the past century. It isn't that feminists have made things better for women but that they've often made things worse. As Teresa points out in the "Be Mindful of Media Message" section, they've often sold girls a bill of goods. Does this mean we don't think women should be doctors and lawyers and professors? Of course not! But we do believe that each woman is called to a vocation and when the voices of radical feminism – with their distinct message of abortion and career at all costs – drone out God's voice to you, well, that is something you want to avoid!

Until rather recently the majority of women commonly followed traditional morality when dating and discerning their vocation in life. You might be a bit young to realize that these choices haven't always panned out real well. Do we believe every woman is called to marriage and motherhood? No, but many are and that call should be embraced, not ignored. Discernment is a process, as JPII had often said, and should start now, while you are a teenager, so that as you mature you will find the joy that God intends you to have and not be confused by chasing the wrong goals in life.

Let's take a look at radical feminism and then we will look at it in the context of Catholic viewpoints. You can be the judge of whether women, as a whole, are better off since the feminist movement began and if you want to get caught up in pursuing false gods.

Here are the main (and very false) precepts of feminism:

- Men and women are interchangeable
- Women's equality with men depends on birth control and abortion rights
- Marriage and family keep women submissive to men

And you thought feminism was all about getting equal pay for equal work! That, we're all for; however, these three points just listed have revealed, over the past couple of decades, the true agenda of radical feminists.

Ladies, you've got to get the real facts. What started out as a movement addressing important issues – like women getting the right to vote – has, in our lifetime, become a Trojan horse. You know the kind: looks like a great gift but is filled with things meant for our harm and not our good.

Today's radical feminists believe that any difference between the sexes have been caused by society and aren't there because of the ways in which the Creator made us. For example, they say that boys play with trucks while girls play with dolls because they have been taught this by the culture. They do not believe men and women are "wired" differently. The only differences are in the body, which are obvious. They do not believe that men and women's brains are different or that they each have separate gifts. The feminists want inclusivity at all costs. So what if a petite woman of 5'1 wants to be a fireman? She can do it. Never mind that she couldn't drag a person down the steps of a burning building let alone do the "fireman's carry." What's the big deal if women want to be in the military and fight in combat? It doesn't matter that she may not have the physical strength to fight or to save a comrade – or that she gets a period. It's all for the cause of inclusivity.

This brings us to the second point. All of this inclusivity, according to drastic feminists, can be ruined by motherhood. Motherhood, they say, wrecks everything. After all, as Scripture wisely warns: you cannot serve two gods – even women with their anti-family agenda know this truth.

Of course a husband and wife may very well decide, together, that both will work; but, even if that is the case, they also both believe that their family comes first and not their individual career goals. A radical feminist doesn't like a woman's family to stand in the way of such things and so discourages a woman from answering her call to motherhood. A radical feminist often suggests that the way to deal with this is to make the woman sterile through surgical sterilization – like tubal ligation – or through artificial birth control. Consider current television ads where a woman touts how wonderful it is to only have 4 periods a year! In this subtle way – or maybe it isn't so subtle if you are really thinking about it – a woman is being discouraged to have children.

Then, if all these attempts to put off motherhood fail, a woman is made to see abortion as a good option. Never mind studies that show abortion has both immediate and long-term negative effects on a woman.

According to feminists with an agenda, women have the right to as many sexual encounters and pleasures as men. If men can do it, so can women! Forget about the fact that women want love and commitment. After all, we're all the same, right?

One of the most radical feminists of the last century was Margaret Sanger, the "mother" of Planned Parenthood. Often, she is mistakenly portrayed as a caring woman who wanted to help poor women control their fertility, thereby alleviating their poverty. In reality, Margaret Sanger was interested in eugenics or ethnic cleansing, much like Hitler. She used the façade of helping poor women to cover the fact that she wanted to rid society of "morons" and undesirables. Even if you wanted to believe in her good intentions, decades later statistics bear out the fact that this thinking has not reduced poverty or helped improve the lives of the poor whatsoever, even though the highest rate of abortion is among poor minorities! Planned Parenthood still has many clinics, today, in poor and impoverished areas.

Ironically, Margaret Sanger was one of eleven children whose mother was a devout Catholic. Sadly, Sanger chose a life that completely contradicted her Catholic roots. Not only did she believe in birth control for others, she herself was known to have had several affairs. This is the heritage of Planned Parenthood.

Thirdly, the feminists we are talking about claim that marriage and family are evil plots to keep women in servitude to men. They say that the family must be abolished and changed. This is why the culture is experiencing social engineering today. The feminists want the definition of family to change to fit the absurd agenda that men and women are interchangeable. This can be seen with gay marriage and gay couples being allowed to adopt. After all, everybody is the same so what's the difference between having a mother and a father or two mothers?

Let's be honest, it must be very confusing to be a guy today! Men have become the enemy to feminists. How sad is that? Men and women were created by God to be helpmates to one another. This is why you must know your faith, girlfriend. The Catholic Church gives the true meaning of feminism. You see and understand, through the Church teachings and writings, that being a female is special and a true gift.

Once you appreciate the Creator's purpose for women, you can truly be a feminist. Remember, Satan is a liar and a deceiver. He takes what God has made and makes up a counterfeit explanation or reason to try and fool mankind; thereby causing souls to be lost. Make no mistake, radical feminism is a lie; a counterfeit of the real thing.

Get the Real Thing, Baby

Let's take the first precept of feminism and see what the Church has to say about it.

1) Men and women are interchangeable.

The Church has always taught that God created man, male and female. He intentionally created them different with each having special gifts. Man is meant to give himself as a gift to woman, and woman receives this gift. In this way, the man and woman are mutual gifts to each other and cooperate in the deepest sense with their purpose which is to know, love and serve God. The Church has always raised woman to a high level of dignity. John Paul's letter on the Dignity and Vocation on Woman states the *"woman must "help" man, and in his turn, he must help her."*

After the fall of man with original sin, man and woman were no longer freely and lovingly giving themselves to one another but were selfish in fulfilling their needs and desires. Specifically, and tragically, man realized he could use woman and woman experienced a deep sense of hurt and betrayal. However, it is imperative to remember that from the beginning, God intended for male and female to be equal in dignity.

Since the fall, however, we have seen that woman has often been taken advantage of and used. From this sad state of affairs, women have tried to remedy the situation by becoming more like men. Of course this accomplished nothing.

JPII stated very clearly that women ought to be very careful not to "masculinize" themselves. JPII understood God's plan and knew that to remedy the wrongs inflicted upon women, both men and women needed to know and understand God's original intention and not the perverse way in which women were becoming "men." JPII spoke of the way in which the loss of feminine originality would "deform and lose what constitutes their [every woman's] essential richness."

Women *are not* interchangeable with men. They think and act different than men. Women are who they are, which is what God intended. In his Letter to Women, John Paul II thanks women for all their contributions to society and just for being women. JPII speaks of the ways in which women can aid humanity in not falling when they respond to the Gospel! It doesn't get better than that!

Many of JPII's writings help us understand that the Catholic Church is a Mother to us all. She will always give you the truth. Hey, consider that the Church is always referred to as "she." Powerful, isn't it?

2) Women's equality with men depends on birth control and abortion rights.

The Church has always taught that man and woman were created with equal dignity. Woman is to be the receiver of love, and as she receives this love, she then gives it away to others. This is called the *"feminine genius."* Woman fulfills her vocation and is truly happy when she gives herself away freely. One of the most beautiful ways that women give themselves away freely is to become a wife and mother.

Let's take a look at the history of birth control in this century. Up until 1931 at the Lambeth Conference, which is an assembly of bishops of the Anglican community, all Christian denominations believed that artificial birth control was immoral and interfered with Natural Law. The Lambeth Conference allowed contraception for married couples who were deemed to have a real and serious reason to use it.

Soon, all denominations – except the Catholic Church – allowed contraception but it was no longer necessary to prove the reason for it was real or serious. The proverbial floodgates to contraception were opened and we can now see that widely used contraception has not improved our society or women's lives even one iota. But the Catholic Church already knew that would be the case because the Church understood what God wanted. Since God doesn't change, He certainly wouldn't say to one generation, "Be fruitful and multiply" but to another generation say, "Use birth control." Right?

Why is the Catholic Church against artificial contraception? When a couple marries and becomes one flesh, their love naturally brings forth life. Procreation and the marital act were never meant to be separated. In the Garden of Eden God told Adam and Eve to be "fruitful and multiply." This is God's design for marriage and for the sexes. By separating the two, God's design is mocked and degraded. In 1968, Pope Paul VI stated in his Encyclical Letter, *Humane Vitae,* (On Human Life), "an act of mutual love which impairs the capacity to transmit life which God the Creator through specific laws has build into it, frustrates His design which constitutes the norm of marriage, and contradicts the will of the Author of life... and is consequently in opposition to the plan of God and His holy will."

Think of it this way. You love food and especially chocolate. However, you are finding that you are putting on weight. You decide you'd better do something to lose this weight. You don't want to give up any of the pleasure you have of eating chocolate. Therefore you decide to binge and purge so that you don't have to take the consequences for your eating habits. Your digestive system was created by God to take in food and process it to be used for the health of the body. You have taken this system and its purposes out of God's plan. If you continue on this path, you will end up experiencing medical problems because of your choices.

The same is true when people decide to use the gift of sexuality in the wrong way. There are many medical consequences to the various types of birth control. The birth control pill has many dangerous side effects that we will discuss later. Birth control, in general, has serious side effects for marriages, for families and for society. In his wisdom, Pope Paul VI predicted what was going to happen if contraception was accepted as a legitimate practice:

- Marital infidelity
- General lowering of moral standards
- Man will forget the reverence due to a woman
- Woman will be reduced to an instrument for the satisfaction of men's desires
- Governments would use forced contraception to achieve their own agendas
- Abortion will become widespread
- Since life is not reverenced, euthanasia will become a standard practice

Wow! Was he smart, or what? All of these predictions came true in only about 40 years!

It's important for you know the facts about the most prominent form of contraception, the birth control pill.

The Pill

A lot of girls and women these days are on the pill, not necessarily for birth control purposes but for "medicinal purposes." Doctors get big kick backs for prescribing the pill from the drug companies. If girls complain of heavy periods or painful periods many doctors put them on the pill.

Let's start from the beginning; Margaret Sanger obtained a grant in 1951 for Dr. Gregory Pincus, a biologist, to research hormonal contraception in order to produce a pill that could be given to women for contraception. During the 1950's Dr. Pincus and Dr. John Rock, an OBGYN, began testing their birth control pill on women. It proved to prevent ovulation in the participants. The doctors then began larger clinical trials to gain approval of the FDA. In 1960 the G.D. Searle drug company got the approval of the FDA to sell the pill as a contraceptive.

In the early years, serious side effects such as blood clots and heart attacks were being publicized. However, instead of taking birth control pills off the market due to these side effects, the FDA made it mandatory that the drug companies include an insert revealing the possible side effects. The drug companies today have changed the dosage of the hormones in the pill; however, the side effects of blood clots and heart attack are still present along with others such as breast cancer, stroke, cervical cancer, infertility and weight gain. If you take a look at the package insert, you will see a list of possible side effects. (American Life League, ThePillKills.com 2008)

The birth control pill works in three ways:

- It stops the functioning of the pituitary gland in the brain, which stops ovulation.
- It interferes with the cervical mucus, making it difficult for the sperm to swim through in order to fertilize the egg.
- It interferes with the lining of the uterus. If there is break-through ovulation and fertilization occurs, it is impossible for a newly fertilized egg, a new human being, to implant into the uterus. The baby is flushed out of the mother's body.

Because of the lower dose of hormones in today's birth control pill, there are more chances of breakthrough ovulation. If this happens, it is possible for the egg to be fertilized, creating a new human life. The mother will be unaware that her new baby is unable to implant and she will unknowingly have an abortion. This is why the pill is called an "abortefecient" drug.

Let's say you're not sexually active, but you are on the pill for heavy and painful menstruation. Take a close look, ladies, at the package insert and see what side effects you may encounter and remember that it is very likely that the serious side effects may not show up for years.

Think about it: the pill takes a healthy system of the body, the female reproductive system, and renders it infertile. What other drug can you think of that is taken to purposely disengage a complete body system? Many women who are on the pill as teens find themselves infertile in their twenties and thirties when they are married and want to start a family. It makes sense though, that if you take a healthy system and put chemicals in it for several years that it may not work correctly afterwards.

Okay, so you have miserable periods. Have you or your parents considered any alternative treatment for your problem? The pill is like a band-aid that covers the problem but does not treat the problem. If you are doubled over in pain during your period, you may have Endometriosis or some other condition. Ask your doctor to look deeper into your condition. You may need a laparoscopy to find out what the problem is. If your doctor finds that your system is healthy, instead of going on the pill:

- Ask for prescription strength ibuprofen
- Ask your doctor about natural progesterone cream
- Ask your doctor about Prometrium, which is natural progesterone in prescription
- Try taking calcium; it is a natural muscle relaxer and many women find that taking 1000 mg. a day will relax the uterus and give relief to cramps
- See if your parents can help you get good nutritional information as this sometimes help alleviate painful cramps
- Do some research on how physical activity can help reduce the pain of periods by getting your body in better condition

Some of these examples come from Paul Hayes OBGYN; Birth Control Pills for Medical Reasons dated October 5, 2005 www.LifeSiteNews .com

Girls, if you are on the pill for "medical reasons" make sure you know the facts about your health and your options. Clinics like Planned Parenthood won't give you all the information you need. Make sure you and your parents discuss the facts and find a pro-life doctor who will be happy to find an alternative for you. Being on the pill can cause health risks to you and may also create a temptation for you if you are dating.

Another thing to consider about the Pill is its link to cancer. According to LifeSiteNews.com, in an August 10, 2005 article, Major U.S. Study Shows Oral Contraceptives Increase Breast

Cancer Risk 44%, the Mayo Clinic journal examined the findings of studies done between 1980-2002. The article finds an increased risk of breast cancer of 44% in pre-menopausal women who were taking the birth control pill before their first pregnancy as compared to women who had not used oral contraceptives. The study re-enforces the 2005 classification of birth control pills as a Type 1 cancer-causing agent to humans. From the same site listed above, another article from October 12, 2005, entitled Cervical Cancer and the Use of Hormone Contraceptives, reports that the birth control pill also increases the risk of cervical cancer.

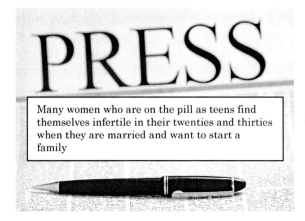

Many women who are on the pill as teens find themselves infertile in their twenties and thirties when they are married and want to start a family

The article states that after 10 years or more of being on the pill, evidence supports the link that the pill does indeed increase the risk of cervical cancer as compared to women who do not use the pill.

The findings of 28 studies showed that the risk of cervical cancer increased by 10% for pill use of less than 5 years. The risk increased to 60% for pill use between 5-9 years and the risk increased 120% for all women using the pill for over 10 years. These are serious facts to be considered when you are considering your options for painful or heavy menstruation, ladies. It may seem like a good idea to get on the pill for "medicinal purposes," but is it worth the risks? The feminist movement is using these chemicals to further their agenda and to promote their second precept: that women are equal to men if they do not allow their bodies to be female, to reproduce.

If all the contraception in the world fails, the feminists rely on abortion on demand. Abortion hurts women and kills babies. Abortion has also been linked to breast cancer and cervical cancer. Get the real truth on such things at sites such as: www.silentnomoreawareness.org and www.priestsforlife.com.

Women suffer from "post-abortion syndrome" and depression when they realize that they have killed their own child through abortion. Many turn to drugs and alcohol to cope with the awful truth. Many post-abortive women experience troubled relationships and lifelong guilt. There really is no way to gather statistics that can fully comprehend how an abortion has lifelong consequences. Yes, feminism is a counterfeit and a lie from the devil

3) Marriage and family will keep women under submission to men.

The Catholic Church elevates motherhood. Through Our Lady, Mary, Catholics revere women and motherhood. John Paul writes in *Mulieris Dignitatem,* "In every age and in every country we find many women, who despite persecution, difficulties and discrimination, have shared in the Church's mission...The witness and achievements of Christian women have had a significant impact on the life of the Church as well as society." Women do this by living their feminine genius, and give themselves away freely to their husbands, families, friends and society.

In the same document, the late Pope writes, "the man was also entrusted by the Creator to the woman – they were entrusted to each other as persons made in the image and likeness of God himself." Man and woman are made for each other. After the fall, man does in fact use woman. However, it was sin that caused this to be so. The Blessed Virgin restored woman's dignity by her "fiat," her yes, to become the mother of God.

All three feminist precepts are lies that can damage a woman's life in untold ways.

The Catholic Church, through her understanding of God's original intention of "different but equal" is the Truth that will set you free! Relying on the Church for the Truth, building your relationship with Jesus and discerning God's will for your life will provide you with great joy and happiness. You will find strength through God's grace and mercy and an ability to experience peace in knowing that you live for God and that His love for you is immense.

Women Living Out Their True Feminine Genius

Mary Ann Glendon

Mary Ann Glendon was selected by the University of Notre Dame as the 2009 recipient of the prestigious Laetare Medal. While initially accepting the honor, Mrs. Glendon ultimately made the difficult and very personal decision to refuse the medal. Her change of mind occurred after the university's scandalous decision to host Barack Obama as the speaker for the 2009 graduation ceremony and give him an honorary award. Glendon considered the honor to Obama to be in violation of the United States Conference of Catholic Bishops' pronouncement that Catholic institutions not give awards or honors to those who go against Catholic moral teaching. Barack Obama is a progressive – and aggressive – pro-choice defender. In a very short time as president of the United States, he has given pro-choice organizations more freedoms and opportunities than any other U.S. president.

Mary Ann was born in 1938 in Massachusetts. She is a pro-life feminist and lives out her feminine genius in both a personal and public way. Her accomplishments and credentials are phenomenal. She is a wife and mother and defender of the faith through such actions as the Notre Dame debacle. She graduated from the University of Chicago Law School and was a professor at Boston College before going to Harvard University. She is the first woman to be President of the Roman Catholic Church's Pontifical Academy of Social Sciences, appointed by Pope John Paul II in 2004.

In 1995 she was the Vatican representative to the international Beijing Conference on Women sponsored by the United Nations. President George W. Bush appointed her to the Presidential Council on Bioethics. She also serves as a consultant to the U.S. Conference of Catholic Bishops Committee on International Policy.

Mary Ann's research has focused on bioethics, human rights, and the theory of law and comparative constitutional law. She lives with her husband Edward. Together they raised three daughters.

Janet Morana

Janet Morana was born in Brooklyn, New York. She has a degree in Foreign Languages, a Master's Degree in Education and a Professional Diploma in Reading. All of these have made her a successful school teacher and in her position as Executive Director of Priests for Life, a pro-life organization that educates clergy and laity on pro-life issues. She has travelled extensively giving presentations on pro-life issues. Janet is a persistent voice for the unborn and a favorite guest on many Catholic radio programs.

Janet also co-founded an organization "Silent No More," with her post-abortive friend. Post-abortive is a term describing any woman who has had an abortion. They wanted to fight the feminist agenda by getting other post-abortive women to publicly tell their stories on how abortion negatively affected their lives. Since then many women have come forward alleviating their own guilt as well as helping other women make decisions to be pro-life. You may have seen women at abortion clinics or pro-life marches carrying signs that say, "I Regret my Abortion," or "Silent No More."

The goals of Janet's organization are:

1. Reach out to people hurt after abortion, encouraging them to attend abortion after-care programs. Invite those who are ready to break the silence by speaking the truth about abortion's negative consequences and the path to healing.

2. Educate the public that abortion is harmful emotionally, physically and spiritually to women, men and families, so that it becomes unacceptable for anyone to recommend abortion as a 'fix' for a problem pregnancy.

3. Share our personal testimonies of hurt and healing to help others avoid the pain of abortion.

Janet Morana is an example of a woman using her gifts to further the Kingdom of God. One person often makes a difference. Think about how you can do the same!

If you've never visited the Vatican's website, do it today! Spend time searching some of the documents written about in *ATG: Truth for Teens*. The Vatican's general website is:

www.Vatican.va

JPII's writings are found at:
http://www.vatican.va/holy_father/john_paul_ii/encyclicals/index.htm

Paul VI's writings are found at:
http://www.vatican.va/holy_father/paul_vi/encyclicals/index.htm

Do it Anyway
A poem by Mother Teresa

People are often unreasonable,
irrational, and self-centered.
Forgive them anyway.

If you are kind, people may accuse
you of selfish, ulterior motives.
Be kind anyway.

If you are successful, you will win
some unfaithful friends and some
genuine enemies.
Succeed anyway.

If you are honest and sincere
people may deceive you.
Be honest and sincere anyway.

What you spend years creating,
others could destroy overnight.
Create anyway.

If you find serenity and happiness,
some may be jealous.
Be happy anyway.

The good you do today
will often be forgotten.
Do good anyway.

Give the best you have,
and it will never be enough.
Give your best anyway.

In the final analysis,
it is between you and God.
It was never between you and them
anyway.

Be Mindful
of the Media
Messages

"I just want to be *skinny*."

That's what I kept telling myself as I turned the pages of *Seventeen Magazine* and admired all the beautiful and bone thin models staring back at me. *Seventeen Magazine,* which as you probably know is still being published today, was just as popular when I was in high school in the mid to late 1970s.

Like most teenage girls, if I wasn't paging through the latest edition of the fashion publication, then my nose was buried in *16 Magazine.* Never heard of it? Well that was my generation's version of today's popular *Teen People. Seventeen Magazine* was all about the fashion and *16 Magazine* was all about fame. You know – the who's who of teen heart throbs and idols. Anybody who was anyone in the movies or television of the late 1960s and 70s (yes I know it seems like we're talking about the dark ages but really we did have magazines and even movies back then) was in *16 Magazine.*

Back in the days before such things as *Teen People,* the Internet, MTV, American Idol and the boatloads of other media choices you have available in the 21st century, *16 Magazine* was the premier place to get the scoop on the stars. Ask your mom or an aunt if they remember singers and actors such as Bobby Sherman, David Cassidy, Davey Jones and, a few years later John Travolta. Those were the hunks and the "it" guys or the Brad Pitts and Jonas Brothers of our era. Eight by ten glossies and color photos of the stars were regularly featured in *"16"* as well as regularly plastered all over the bulletin boards (remember this is long before pages on MySpace and Facebook) bedroom walls and bathroom mirrors.

And that's exactly why I wanted to be skinny. I know it sounds far-fetched, but I had convinced myself that by being skinny I could experience the glamour of those thin, gorgeous models in *Seventeen Magazine* and then I might even be able to attract a boyfriend as cute as Bobby Sherman or David Cassidy! The possibilities were limitless!

One of the models I admired so much – Susan Dey – actually went from the cover of *Seventeen* to a coveted spot on the hit show "The Partridge Family," co-starring with David Cassidy. How lucky could a girl get? And *every* girl my age wanted to look like Susan and be Susan, if only the heavens were granting such miracles! I was no exception. Susan Dey was tall and thin with long dark hair.

Unfortunately, about the only thing I had in common with Susan was the hair color. But that would soon change. Little did I know that we would soon share a similar struggle with a newly diagnosed eating disorder.

That's why it is so important to discern the messages that are coming at you. When you look in the mirror, you need to see yourself first and foremost as a child of Christ, a daughter of the King who is His most precious creation. Although I was raised in a good Catholic home and went to an excellent Catholic grade school, the pull of the culture, at times, was too strong for me to resist. That's why magazine images and a TV show, along with plenty of peer pressure, sent me over the edge in terms of losing control of my eating habits. Again, there was no Internet, no iPhone or iPod, no cable TV, DVD's, YouTube, texting, or MySpace. We had a handful of magazines, radio stations, and TV shows to choose from and I was still so heavily influenced by the media that the influence turned into an obsession that eventually led to my being hospitalized.

I have always struggled with my weight, as long as I can remember. When I was about 11 or 12 years old I was tired of the teasing and asked my Mom if I could go on a diet and lose a few pounds. Off we went to the pediatrician who agreed a few pounds yes, maybe 10 pounds would be a healthy decision for me; but I had to follow her instructions and eat well-balanced healthy meals, a little less bread and pasta and a little more fruits and veggies. Nothing more. Nothing less.

It worked. I lost the weight. I looked better and felt better about myself but it wasn't enough. I thought "if I can lose ten pounds, what's ten more?" And so I kept dieting and I kept losing more and more weight. My parents tried to get me to eat but it was no use. By this time I was thirteen years old and about to graduate from grade school. Boys were finally beginning to notice me and others were paying more attention to me as well. I was willing to put up with the family arguments over food. My new look was worth it, or so I thought.

That was until the pediatrician told my parents it was time to have me examined by local experts who were just learning about eating disorders with strange names such as Anorexia Nervosa and Bulimia. Anorexia Nervosa is a psychological illness mostly affecting young women and girls and results in abnormal eating behaviors and excessive weight loss. Bulimia involves bouts of binge eating followed by self-induced vomiting. Both disorders can be extremely harmful to your body causing, in some cases, long term damage due to malnutrition and other strains on the organs and normal bodily functions.

Speaking from personal experience, an eating disorder is nothing to play around with and if you think you or someone you know may be suffering from an eating disorder; or, if someone in your circle of family and friends is becoming obsessed with dieting or appearance, talk to an adult and seek help for that person who may not be able to seek it herself. Sadly, you probably know of at least one person in your school or neighborhood with an eating disorder, at least that's what the research says. According to ANRED, the Anorexia Nervosa and Related

Eating Disorders organization, more than half of today's teens are on diets. The average age for a girl in this country to start dieting is eight years old, and if that's not shocking or sad enough for you, more than 80 percent of 10-year-old American girls say they are afraid of becoming fat.

 If that's not bad enough, guess what the most popular high school graduation gift is for girls? Maybe you're thinking gals are hoping for some cash to put toward college or maybe some dorm room furniture or supplies? Lots of young women hope for a trip to Europe or a new or used set of wheels to help them get to and from campus or a summer job. But none of those gift ideas top the list. Surveys today show plastic surgery – as in breast augmentations – come in as the number one graduation present for today's young women!

And if you think we women wise up as we get older, guess again. In a recent study, the American Society of Plastic Surgeons found that today's working women think it's plastic surgery that will help them in today's competitive job market. That's right; 73 percent said it's youthful appearance and beauty that will impact their success, not experience, hard work or an advanced degree.

When I was hospitalized at Children's Hospital of Michigan I weighed in at about 85 pounds. My periods, which began when I was 11 and had become regular before the obsessive dieting, had stopped completely. I was weak and miserable most of the time. I thought I looked like a million bucks when, in reality, I looked more like a million bones. When I looked in the mirror I saw someone who looked more like Susan from *Seventeen* than plain old chubby Teresa from suburban Detroit.

I was eager to start high school, especially with my brand new look. But I was then told that being hospitalized could change my plans. If I didn't gain weight, my pediatrician and the other doctors would recommend I be kept out of school for health reasons. Since Anorexia and Bulimia were new diagnoses there was little counseling or help available for sufferers like myself. We just had to move on and do what we were told. The threat of missing out on high school was enough to gradually whip me back into shape. But I have never been the same. That was more than three decades ago and I still suffer at least some long-term consequences from my bout with Anorexia, both physically and psychologically.

Physically, since my body was affected at such an important stage developmental-wise, I have had some female issues which doctors say could be tied to the eating disorder. While I am not a psychiatrist or an M.D., it's been my own personal experience that an eating disorder always stays with you even though most of the time I am able to maintain my weight and eat healthy. I exercise and take good care of myself; but, there are days that I still obsess way too much about food and eating or not eating. And remember that this is more than 30 years after my bout with Anorexia! Trying to live up to an image on TV, or in a magazine, which is simply a lie, is not worth your time and especially your health. Remember the actress/model I admired so much and tried to emulate? Well, many years later I would learn that Susan Dey was also anorexic and she was struggling with the illness while she was gracing the cover of all the magazines and starring in a hit sitcom.

Don't get me wrong. There is absolutely nothing wrong with wanting to look your best. And, in fact, you should want to care about your body. Scripture tells us our bodies are temples of the Holy Spirit. But we need to apply this teaching with a healthy approach and that means moderation. If you are concerned about your weight, talk to your parents and see about sitting down with your doctor. He or she will be able to give you a good assessment of the best weight for your age and height. Never go on a diet or take any type of dieting products without your parents' input as well as the input of medical experts. Your doctor can also give you some idea of the best foods to fuel your body as well as an appropriate exercise plan. Listen to the experts and those who love you, namely the Lord and your family. If you don't you could end up struggling with a lifetime of weight and health issues. And remember, I am speaking not only from my background as a media expert who speaks and writes books on media issues but as a former Anorexic!

Perception Is Not Reality!

When I looked at a picture of my idol, Susan Dey, or watched her on TV, I perceived that she was perfect and had the perfect life. But I was wrong on several fronts. Not only was I to learn years later about her battle with Anorexia; but, as I went to college and studied TV and communications – and subsequently started working in the secular media – I learned that it is easy to portray a certain image on camera or in print to give the viewer or reader a certain perception of the person they're looking at or reading about. I learned that perception – when it comes to the television set, the computer, or the big Hollywood movie screen – is definitely *not* reality. So much can be done with lighting, camera angles, editing, and air-brushing. Today, with the advances in computer technology, well, the sky is the limit.

In addition to hours spent with a make-up artist and hair stylists, glam shots in magazines or on billboards are often altered to make the model or celebrity appear to have bigger eyes, fuller lips, or a longer, thinner nose. And that's just for starters. Other tricks of the trade can also make unwelcome blemishes or cellulite magically disappear, with the click of a computer mouse!

If a celebrity is caught on camera, naturally, without all the fuss and muss they are more like you and I than they would like us to believe. Don't believe me?

About two years ago, actress Jennifer Love Hewitt was caught on camera in a bathing suit by one of the tabloids. Now even though Hewitt is very attractive and thin, she is not perfect. And since this wasn't a scheduled photo shoot or publicity event, the picture was less than flattering. It was quickly plastered all over the tabloids and the Hollywood gossip magazines untouched or altered. As a result, this lovely woman, who happens to be a size two, was labeled fat and out of shape by the paparazzi. The girl is a size 2 for goodness sake and she was insulted and mocked in the press because she was snapped in her normal everyday surroundings.

Here is another case of perception not being reality. Just because a person has a few imperfect bumps or lumps doesn't mean they aren't beautiful – on the inside and the outside! If this is how they treat a major star, then no wonder so many young people, especially teen girls, have body image issues.

Ever wonder just how many messages out there add to body image or self-esteem issues of today's women and girls? Well here are just a few more statistics:
- One out of every four TV commercials contains a message about appearance.
- 80 percent of women questioned by *People Magazine* said media images make them feel insecure.
- More than 50 percent of women in an international survey agreed that attractive women are more valued by men.
- One-third of the women say they are somewhat dissatisfied with their bodies – and diet products rake in billions a year because of that.
- One out of every three women is on a diet at any given time.

These statistics don't even begin to scratch the surface when it comes to being bombarded by cultural influences. Is it any surprise that so many of us struggle with ourselves each time we look in the mirror? But it doesn't have to be this way.

You are royalty. You are a daughter of the King of Kings. Deep down you may know that but do you really "get it?" I know that I didn't. It has taken me years of going through what I like to call cultural de-tox, or cultural rehab, in order to develop a healthy self-esteem.

Not only does our society tell teen girls and women they have to look a particular way, be a particular size and wear just the right outfits in order to be accepted; but, our culture also tells women that their freedom is tied in with their sexuality and then, later on, with their professional success outside the home. What they say is: "You're not somebody until you accept a certain lifestyle and earn a big enough pay check."

Success in the secular arena has nothing to do with who you are inside as in your relationship with Christ, your character or family ties. It's in the career choice and the collection of boyfriends or encounters that show the world you have "arrived." The only problem is those worldly types of pursuits are roads that lead to dissatisfaction and lots of dead ends. I know as here again I am speaking from experience.

Teresa's Testimony

By now you're probably thinking *"Hello. Earth to Teresa! When is this lady going to get a clue?"* Well, unfortunately some of us are a lot more stubborn than others and although I eventually was able to combat an eating disorder, I still had a disordered way of thinking about a lot of other things. I was able to re-gain my physical health but my spiritual health was greatly lacking. Back in the 70s, when I graduated from Catholic grade school, there was little or no faith formation that followed. It's not like today where you have great organizations such as Pure Fashion or Life Teen. We didn't have youth groups or youth conferences. Most of the faith formation was left up to our parents who brought us up as their parents did, saying our prayers and going to Mass once a week. Prayer and weekly Mass are both a must, of course, but if we're not doing much in between – such as reading Scripture, praying with our family, going through our daily examination of conscience, as well as receiving the Sacraments on a regular basis – then our relationship with God will suffer. Our egos, and the influences of the world, will take over. We figure we're fine on our own or with what we are doing. I always like to think of the word "ego" as an acronym as in "easing God out." And that is exactly what I did.

Once I was out of the hospital and in high school, it quickly again became all about me. I had my goals and by golly I was going to reach them. And I did just that, and at a very fast pace. My ego was fed well. I worked on the high school radio station and newspaper. I was on the forensics team and won speaking awards. Then it was graduation and off to college where I pursued my journalism career with great self-determination and no direction from God. Who needed Him? Or so I thought.

I was having a lot of success and even more fun doing things on my own. God would only have been a kill-joy. By the time the end of my first semester of college rolled around I was what's known as a "C & E" Catholic – a "Christmas and Easter Catholic." Oh, sure, once in a while I would head to the campus Catholic parish if I needed a favor from God. That was usually the night before a big exam. But other than that it was me, myself, and I.

Mass was something to do with the family when I went home for the holidays. This was the late 70s and early

80s, about 10 to 15 years after the sexual revolution and the women's liberation movement had taken hold. Feminism was becoming the order of the day for women. In retrospect, it is easy to see that the hijacking of the movement by radical feminists could only lead to pain and suffering for a multitude of women, especially Catholic women. You see, despite what some may tell you, the Catholic Church was not opposed to feminism. The Church wanted women to embrace a new kind of feminism where men and women worked together in collaboration for the good of society and God's Kingdom -- instead of a radical feminism that pitted male against female and often did its best to re-label marriage and children as bondage verses blessings for women.

I bought into a lot of those lies and became a headstrong career woman. I excelled in journalism, graduating with awards and honors having both earned my degree as well as had several job internships under my belt. The college internships led to getting hired at a local radio station in my hometown of Detroit. Marriage was never part of my agenda but thanks be to God, the Lord had other ideas for me. I was blessed enough to meet a wonderful man and get married; but, I wasn't going to let marriage stop me from pursuing my career goals of being a star reporter. I allowed myself to believe that our marriage would take care of itself and that as long as we loved each other we would be just fine.

No surprise that we soon had a lot of challenges. After getting married in the Catholic Church, we pretty much pushed God to the sidelines. We were both career-oriented and fixated on getting all the things the world said was important: money, professional status and a new home. I was convinced that if I put more emphasis on family and home, opportunities in broadcasting would pass me by. My husband agreed and before we knew it, we were what is known as "married singles" – married in the eyes of God and the law but single in lifestyle.

The ironic thing is that, despite all of the material success, we weren't really happy. We were never satisfied and kept looking for more. Maybe a bigger house, more money or more journalism awards would make a difference. On the outside we looked like the perfect couple. I had made it in the news business in my own hometown. My husband was climbing up the corporate ladder at his firm, but something or someone was missing – and that was God.

God did come back into our lives, but very slowly. My husband was invited to a men's Bible study through a mutual friend. The Bible study made my husband realize what was missing in our lives and he began to study the Catholic faith at a local seminary. He also recommitted his life to Christ and the Church. It took me (you know, the hard-headed one) a lot longer. The Lord had to knock me off my high horse in order to get my attention. The high horse happened to be a TV news job, which I coveted. The news media had become my "god" at the expense of my husband, family and friends.

Like all false gods, this one let me down. One day I was reporting the top story for the evening news and the next day I was standing in the unemployment line. It was then that I began to realize that my priorities needed a major adjustment.

Thanks to lots of prayer and a faithful, loving spouse I found my way back to God. I eventually found myself back in the secular news media and then a few years later the Lord brought me into the Catholic media – where I still am today – and onto the Christian speaker's circuit. I've never been happier or felt more fulfilled.

Choices and Challenges

One of my favorite presentations that I give as a speaker is one entitled *"Choices and Challenges Facing Today's*

Teens." It's targeted toward young people your age and includes much of the testimony I just shared in the previous pages. It's meant to show how the choices we make in life, and the challenges we face, can have both positive and negative effects on our lives depending on, of course, how we handle them.

You've already read how my challenges with an eating disorder, as well as my choice to put my career first, had negative consequences. But the biggest mistake I made along the way was allowing my ego (remember "easing God out") to take control. It was *"my will be done"* as opposed to *"thy will be done."* When I was growing up, more "choices" were becoming available to women both in the areas of education and in the job market. One saying I heard constantly back in the 70s was *"women belong in the house and the senate."* That was meant not only to stress the need for more women in politics – which is fine and probably true – but also to poke fun or demean women who chose to stay home – which is just plain wrong. I didn't realize until much later in life that the radical feminists were only for "choice" if the choices met their specific definition and that usually didn't include marriage and raising a family. That's quite a limited definition of choice, don't you think?

But choices are important. Consider how God has given you free will to make your own choices throughout your life. But you must consider that along with more freedom comes more responsibility. If you believe what the music videos, the movies, the news media and the magazines are telling you, then you'll be settling for damaging messages and making poor choices. In other words, you risk believing the lies that you need to live up to certain images or ideals.

A 2007 survey of 18-to-25-year olds said "getting rich" was their number one goal in life. Their second goal, for 51 percent of those questioned in the same report, was "being famous." Another study, this one conducted in 2009 by the University of Rochester in New York, found that fame, fortune and beauty are not all that they're cracked up to be. One of the researchers said that although our culture puts a strong emphasis on attaining wealth and fame, *"pursuing these goals does not contribute to having a satisfying life."* The study found that what really matters is *"having loving relationships and contributing to the community."* Sounds an awful lot like the Bible doesn't it? Jesus is always telling us that it is not all about us. If we want to save our lives and be happy, we have to lose our lives for His sake. And as that famous prayer of St. Francis reminds us, *"it is in the giving that we receive."* It's great to have options but we have to make the right choices.

Liberated by God's Love

One of my dear friends, who is also a wonderful priest and Bible teacher, reminds his congregation often that the world tends to see Jesus and the Catholic Church as some big celestial stick-in-the-mud just waiting to stop all of our fun, when just the opposite is true. He was reiterating something the Holy Father Pope Benedict XVI said during a talk to young people in 2006:

"Faith and Christian ethics do not wish to suffocate love but to make it healthy and strong and really free. This is precisely the meaning of the Ten Commandments which are not a series of "no's" but a big "yes" to love and to life."

The Bible tells us in the Old Testament Book of Jeremiah 29:11 *"for I know the plans I have for you says the Lord. Plans not to harm you. Plans to give you hope and a future."* Jesus tells us in the Gospel of St. John 10:10 *"I have come to give them life that they may have it abundantly."* Does this sound like a God who is holding out on us?

A great way to find out just how liberating God's love is, especially when it comes to the dignity of women, is to read His word in the Bible and see how Jesus always treated women equally and with great respect. In his 1998 document *"On the Dignity and Vocation of Women,"* Pope John Paul II quoted the Gospels to explain how Jesus was a "promoter" of women. (The emphasis on the text is mine.)

"It is universally admitted - even by people with a critical attitude towards the Christian message - that in the eyes of his contemporaries Christ became a promoter of women's true dignity and of the vocation corresponding to this dignity. At times this caused wonder, surprise, often to the point of scandal: "They marveled that he was talking with a woman" (Jn 4:27), because this behavior differed from that of his contemporaries.

Even Christ's own disciples "marveled." The Pharisee to whose house the sinful woman went to anoint Jesus' feet with perfumed oil "said to himself, 'If this man were a prophet, he would have known who and what sort of woman this is who is touching him, for she is a sinner'" (Lk 7:39).

Even greater dismay, or even "holy indignation," must have filled the self-satisfied hearers of Christ's words: "the tax collectors and the harlots go into the Kingdom of God before you" (Mt 21:31).

In all of Jesus' teaching, as well as in his behavior, one can find nothing which reflects the discrimination against women prevalent in his day. On the contrary, his words and works always express the respect and honor due to women.

As a journalist, one of the first things I learned was to always consider the source. So when it comes to discovering what God and the Church says, go to *the* sources: the Bible and countless Church documents. This way we know what the Church and Scripture actually teach us verses the world's very skewed version of things.

Take, as another excellent example of Church teaching, John Paul II's 1995 *Letter to Women*. He wanted women to know that the Church was not turning its back on the concerns being expressed by women around the world regarding equality.

> *When it comes to setting women free from every kind of exploitation and domination, the Gospel contains an ever relevant message which goes back to the attitude of Jesus Christ himself. Transcending the established norms of his own culture, Jesus treated women with openness, respect, acceptance and tenderness. In this way he honored the dignity which women have always possessed according to God's plan and in his love.*
>
> *...And what shall we say of the obstacles which in so many parts of the world still keep women from being fully integrated into social, political and economic life? We need only think of how the gift of motherhood is often penalized rather than rewarded, even though humanity owes its very survival to this gift. Certainly, much remains to be done to prevent discrimination against those who have chosen to be wives and mothers. As far as personal rights are concerned, there is an urgent need to achieve real equality in every area: equal pay for equal work, protection for working mothers, fairness in career advancements, equality of spouses with regard to family rights and the recognition of everything that is part of the rights and duties of citizens in a democratic State.*

In the *Gospel of Life*, John Paul II continues:

In transforming culture so that it supports life, women occupy a place in thought and action which is unique and decisive. It depends on them to promote a "new feminism" which rejects the temptation of imitating models of "male domination" in order to acknowledge and affirm the true genius of women in every aspect of the life of society and overcome all discrimination, violence and exploitation.

One of the greatest gifts we have as women is to be able to bring new life into the world. But the world, as Pope John Paul II indicated in his letter to women, tends to see that gift as a burden that needs to be controlled, or removed, as in birth control and abortion.

Our highly secular and over-sexualized culture tells us we should be able to do whatever we want with whomever and whenever we want, regardless of the consequences. Even, according to the secular world, if that means resorting to violence – such as the ending of a human life through an abortion. Some methods of contraception, such as the birth control pill or the IUD (intrauterine device), can cause abortions.

Many women's organizations, with backing from the mainstream media, place all of these evils in the category of "choice." But, remember earlier when I said they want you to have choices but only if you choose their agenda? This is why you ought to be cautious and aware of media messages.

An average teen, in terms of media consumption, spends 40 plus hours a week on-line, watching TV, listening to music etc. Here's just a sample of the many messages about so called "choices" you're receiving:
- 70 percent of all TV programming contains sexual content
- Young people view at least 14 thousand sexual messages a year on TV alone

- 75 percent of the videos on MTV contain sexual imagery
- More than half of the videos on MTV contain violence
- Over one thousand studies in the United States show at least a casual connection between violence in the media and aggressive behavior in children
- At least 10 percent of youth violence is attributed to violence on TV

The world wants you to think that all of this leads to freedom and happiness. But what it really leads to as you can see here is a lot of problems:

- One out of four sexual active teens will contract an STD by the time they graduate high school
- Sex on TV is linked to higher pregnancy rate among teens
- 22 percent of teen girls admit to sexting – which is sending suggestive pictures of themselves over the Internet usually via cell phone or texting
- Young people between the ages of 13 and 17 are sending or receiving an average of more than 17 hundred text messages a month
- One third of today's teens have talked to strangers on-line
- Use of the Internet is a contributing factor in nearly 50 percent of all family, relationship and family problems
- 11 percent of the people going on-line are becoming compulsive or addicted

The world wants us to believe that God is all about oppression and that if we follow His plan, rather than our plan, we will be miserable. This sounds awfully familiar. Pull out your Bible and read the first few Chapters of the Old Testament Book of Genesis.

This is the same lie the serpent told Eve: that God was holding out and if they went ahead and defied God, and ate from the tree of the knowledge of good and evil, they would be just like God. What happened when they turned their backs on God?

We know that's when we have the entrance of original sin. Adam and Eve wanted to be like God and thought they could "choose" or determine good and evil for themselves. But God is God and we are not. And if we would just stop and connect all the dots, we would see just how harmful trying to play God with our own lives and the lives of others can be.

It's not all that complicated, after all. God has a plan. He is our Father and the Creator of everything and He knows what is best for us and how that plan should work. As you can see in the personal experiences I've shared with you, along with some of the statistics provided in this section, turning our backs on God is not in our best interest. We do, of course, have free will or a "choice" to make. But choices come with moral and often physical and psychological consequences, which the world often "chooses" to ignore. Clever, huh?!

As we pointed out, the culture with the help of thousands of media messages claims that sex is nothing more than a thing to be used for personal gratification. God and the Church tell us that sex is sacred and meant only for marriage and to bring new life into the world. Viewing sex as another form of recreation leads to the probability of STDs and unexpected pregnancies. It also leads to the objectification of women, broken relationships, the loss of life through abortion and contraception and, most importantly, the separation from God.

It's hard to wrap our minds around the statistics in terms of the impact sexual promiscuity and immorality has had on society; however, many government agencies, such as the Centers for Disease Control and Prevention, as well as the Gutmacher Institute (the former research arm of

Planned Parenthood) along with professional medical organizations have confirmed these concerns:

- 50 million lives have been lost through legalized abortion
- Abortion is the number once cause of death among African Americans with 13 million African American babies lost so far through abortion
- Abortion is connected to increased rates of drug abuse, alcohol abuse, and psychological problems among post-abortive women
- Abortion is connected to an increase in domestic problems among post-abortive women including domestic violence, child abuse and divorce
- Sexually transmitted diseases or STDs are at epidemic proportions in this country, especially among young women with 19 million STD infections reported annually

Even the American Psychological Association agrees that media messages being sold to young women can be damaging and lead to an increase in eating disorders and other problems. The APA report released in 2007 entitled *"The Sexualization of Girls"* found that these problems occur when:

- A girl's value comes only from her sexual appeal to the exclusion of other characteristics
- A person is held to a standard that equates physical attractiveness with being sexy
- Sexuality is inappropriately imposed upon a person

The APA found that all types of media contribute to these problems and they even pointed to items such as *Bratz* dolls and suggestive clothing, along with pop stars such as Madonna and others, as having a negative influence on young women and causing them to feel like objects rather than real people.

Ironically, or maybe not so ironically, the APA report sounded a lot like something the Catholic Church said over 40 years ago. It was contained in an encyclical written by then Pope Paul VI. Many consider this document one of the most prophetic Church writings ever given to us when you consider what the late Pope discussed in *"Humanae Vitae."* He warned of a major decline in morality and also saw women being objectified by an over sexualized culture that would do its best to get rid of God.

> *Let them first consider how easily this course of action could open wide the way for marital infidelity and a general lowering of moral standards. Not much experience is needed to be fully aware of human weakness and to understand that human beings—and especially the young, who are so exposed to temptation—need incentives to keep the moral law, and it is an evil thing to make it easy for them to break that law.*

> *It is also to be feared that the man, growing used to the employment of anti-conceptive practices, may finally lose respect for the woman and, no longer caring for her physical and psychological equilibrium, may come to the point of considering her as a mere instrument of selfish enjoyment, and no longer as his respected and beloved companion.*

> *Paragraph 17 Humanae Vitae*

As you can see, even though the medical and scientific experts might not realize it or want to admit it, science and research eventually back up God's plan. All of the pain and misery outlined through countless studies (not to mention lots of personal experience, including my own) can be avoided if we follow God's plan for life, marriage and human sexuality.

There is a reason this book is entitled *"Truth for Teens."* We want you to know *the* truth as in Jesus Christ and the

Catholic Church. The Lord says *"I am the way, the truth, and the life. No one comes to the Father except through me."* He also tells us, *"the truth will set you free."* But God is also a gentleman. He won't force Himself on us. In the Book of Revelation Jesus says, *"Behold I stand at the door and knock. If anyone opens it I will come in and dine with him."* Jesus will never take away our free will. We can *"choose"* to say *"yes"* to Him and real happiness and *"no"* to the lies of the world that lead to chaos and destruction.

"I put before you life and death. Choose Life."

Take it from Teresa – Top Three Media Tips for Today's Savvy Teens

1. Think WWJW!

A few years ago there was
a very popular saying in Christian circles. It was actually more of a question to keep believers on their toes: What Would Jesus Do?

Often you would see this on a pin, a bracelet, or a bumper sticker. And it was a reminder for Christians to always do their best to live out the faith no matter where they were or what they were doing. It was a slogan that caught on among Christian teens as they did their best to stand up for their faith amidst growing peer pressure and cultural influences.

Given some of the issues I've pointed out regarding media influences, I think it's a great idea to alter that popular phrase or slogan just a bit when it comes to our media habits. How about asking ourselves when we sit down at the TV, go to the movies with some friends, or go on-line; WWJW? Or What Would Jesus Watch? I even tell families and others who attend my seminars to place a statue or an image of Jesus and or the Blessed Mother near the TV set and the computer to remind us that God should be first in our lives and viewing something that does not support our families is an insult to the Lord and His Church and also can lead to problems in our own lives if we find ourselves allowing the media messages to affect the way we think and act. So remember "WWJW" and ask yourself "What Would Jesus Watch?"

2. Take a Media Reality Check!

Did you ever stop and think about how much media you consume each week? Most young people your age are spending more than 40 hours a week using media outlets with the most time spent on-line and watching television. Stop and think about that for a minute. More than 40 hours a week means that the media usage in your life is comparable to a full-time job! And considering that the content is not exactly faith or family-friendly you have to wonder who really needs that much time in front of the TV or computer screen?

While the media can be very helpful when it comes to researching for homework or keeping in touch with friends and even providing great resources for our Catholic faith we have to use the media in moderation. If you are spending even close to that amount of time with various media outlets, how much time is that leaving for your relationship with the Lord? So that's where the media reality check comes in. This is something I suggest in my books and media presentations. Sit down with your parents and have an honest discussion about the media and ask each other three very important questions:

- ✞ How are my media habits impacting my relationship with God?
- ✞ How are my media habits impacting my relationship with family?
- ✞ Am I willing to do something about media influences?

By answering these questions you and your family should be able to come up with a healthy media action plan. If you don't spend a lot of family face-to-face time together – family members are off in their own space working on the computer or watching TV – these are good indications that some things need to change. Why not take the lead on this and offer to help your parents come up with a plan, especially if you have younger brothers or sisters? Did you know that the American Academy of Pediatrics actually has a policy stating no TV for children under two years of age? That's how concerned medical experts are about the influence of TV. For young people your age the AAP says no more than two hours a day of television. The AAP also stresses that the TV and the computer should be in the central area of the home where usage can be monitored. Help your family get closer to Jesus and the Church by setting an example and offering to cut down on your own media consumption.

3. Turn Off All The Media Noise Just One Night a Week!

That's right. No TV, no Internet, no cell phones, or radios. Go media-free just one night a week. This suggestion comes from one of the greatest Catholic leaders we have in the Church today: Archbishop Charles J. Chaput, from Denver. You may have seen him on Catholic television or heard about him from your parish priest. That's because Archbishop Chaput is not only a wonderful shepherd to his flock in Denver but he is also a prominent speaker, teacher, and author who frequently addresses cultural issues. He has spoken quite a bit recently on media influence especially as it pertains to Catholics and the formation of conscience.

He recently addressed the American Bible Society in New York telling those in attendance that too many of us are *"happy with our complacency, vanity, compromises, comfort, and bad formation."* Then he went on to make this very good suggestion for Catholic families.

> *One of the best things we can do for our own faith is to simply turn off the noise around us* **<u>one night a week</u>**. *Computers, televisions, cell phones, DVD players, radios, and iPods-turn them all off. Not every night.* **<u>Just one night</u>**. *This is a very fruitful habit to borrow from Mormon families; one night a week spent reading, talking with each other and praying over Scripture. We can at least do that much. And if we do, we will discover that eventually we're sober again and not drunk on technology and our own overheated appetites.*

Just think about all the fruit that could come from you and your family being media-free for just one night a week! What a great example you and your family could set for other families in your neighborhood and parish!

So why not go for it? As a daughter of the King you deserve better than the message the majority of the media outlets are sending you. Jesus has given you so much. Why not say "thank you" to God by giving Him one night a week of your complete, media-free attention?

Tune out the media and tune into God instead. You'll be glad you did!

One night a week your family should pray together, play together and stay together!

Fashion

Every girl has her own unique style. When a person wears all black including her fingernails, hair and eye makeup, it says something about her, doesn't it? The girl who presents herself like this gives the impression of being hard, tough and/or depressed. What about the girl who wears her clothing skin tight and shows cleavage? What is she saying about herself? "Pay attention to me," "I don't respect myself," "I am loose with my affection," "I want someone to love me." Those are the things that a girl is saying whether she knows it or not – or whether she intends it or not. You see, the way you look tells a story about you and makes an impression on others. You will be judged on how you look, right or wrong. You make judgments about people all the time even though you may not realize it.

Fashion is a way to communicate something about you.

Did you know it only takes six seconds to make a first impression? Yep, that's it. You never get a second chance at a first impression. Yes, people change their minds about those they have met once they get better acquainted but you may never get the opportunity for that.

You only get one chance to make a good first impression. You are a daughter of the King. You are royalty and should cherish your princess role!

Here are a few ways you can always bring about a good first impression.

- ✝ Wear clothing that fits well and correctly
- ✝ Wear classic styles
- ✝ Cover your private areas such as cleavage, midriff and buttocks
- ✝ Wear a flattering and modern hairstyle and appropriate makeup
- ✝ Avoid piercings and tattoos as these do nothing to speak to your dignity
- ✝ Take the time to say something to whomever you meet – don't just say "Hi" but say "Hello! It is nice to meet you!"

Making the right impression may land you the job you want, will help you make the kind of friends that have the same values as you have, and if your vocation is marriage, will attract the kind of man that is worthy of you. Do you ever go fishing, or have a father, grandfather or brother who does? Not that fishing is popular with a lot of teenage girls, but it makes for a good analogy, so bear with me here. When fishing, there are different types of lures and bait used to catch certain kinds of fish.

It's the same concept, ladies, when it comes to "fishing for a man." Come on, let's not pretend that women don't do that! If you are a healthy teen, you should be attracted to the opposite sex. That's normal. If your vocation is marriage, you very well will be "fishing for a man" at some point. Make sure you use the correct bait so that you will attract the Hard Worker, the Brainiac or the Nice Guy. Otherwise you may find yourself dredging up the Octopus, the Bum or the Bad Boy. The Bad Boy or Bum may seem exciting and thrilling at first, but will end up causing you nothing except heartache and pain.

The important thing is to keep all the attention on your face. This is done by covering the bust, midriff and bottom appropriately. When you wear necklaces, earrings and or tastefully done makeup, you are bringing the attention of others to your face and eyes. This is where you want others to look because it's said that the eyes are the windows to the soul. This is the way to make a good first impression.

Good manners also aid in giving the best impression of you, a daughter of the King. "Hey" is not an appropriate greeting. Communication skills are just as important as the clothing you wear when making an impression. With technology taking over person-to-person communication, many young people have completely lost the ability to converse with each other face to face. This is not good!

Fashion and Modesty

Many people picture pioneer-style clothing when they hear the word "modesty." Nothing could be further from the truth. Modesty is beautiful, fashionable, stylish and holds mystery. It guides how one looks at and behaves towards another person. So if you are wearing a V-neck halter-top, which reveals your back, shoulders and cleavage, you are revealing far too much. And be assured that guys will be imagining what the rest looks like. By covering yourself, you allow others to see you as a person and not just "boobs," "butt" or "legs." How do you feel if a guy looks at your bust line when he talks to you? Hopefully you recognize that you are not being taken seriously – because you aren't!

The *Catechism of the Catholic Church* teaches that modesty protects the intimate center of the person and it means to refuse to unveil what should remain hidden.

Help others to focus on the real "you" by wearing garments that cover your cleavage and other intimate parts. If you are relying on your body to get you attention, you'll get it all right, but truly, deep down is that what you really want?

You are worth more than a rare jewel and, sister; you don't need the wrong type of attention. Once you realize that, you will be free, you will know who you are in Christ Jesus.

The fashion industry, unfortunately, is not interested in your dignity or any other woman's dignity. It is about the almighty dollar. That's right. They only care about making money. That's why things in fashion change so quickly, especially in the Junior's market. The industry uses advertising to sell the style they are pushing for the season. Nothing is really new in fashion. The industry just recycles every once in awhile. This is why moms sometimes laugh at what their daughters wear – because they had worn it first, many years before! (Is it difficult to imagine mom being fashionable?) The fabric may change or there may be a detail or two that is different but everything you see in the stores has been done before.

Here are a few examples:

✟ Platform shoes were popular in the 1940s and 1970s

✟ Fitted bodices were in style in the 1950s

✟ Drop-waist blouses and dresses were all the rage in the 1920s

✟ Knee-length dresses and skirts were popular in the 1940s

✟ Pointed-toe stilettos were in style in the 1950s

✟ Fur coats and collars were the big thing in the 1930s

✟ The 1970s brought in the "hobo" look with baby doll tops and dresses

✟ Leggings were popular in the 1960s and the 1980s

✟ Argyle was in style in the 1950's and the 1980s

✟ The 1930s brought in long-fitted skirts

✟ High-waisted pleated trousers were worn in the 1940s and 1970s

✟ Skinny jeans and long sweaters were worn in the 1980s

✟ The 1970s made low-riding jeans and halter tops popular

And you thought all the styles in the stores were new! Nope, nothing in fashion is really new. Usually the cycle for an item is about thirty years; so, if you keep things long enough, you'll be able to wear them again in thirty years.

One thing to realize about fashion is that you, the consumer, have power. What doesn't sell in the stores will not stick around, so it is important for you to help shape the fashion market by your buying patterns. Take, as an example, the low-riding jeans. They became popular in the 1990s and are still being sold today. If enough consumers stop buying these, other options will appear in the stores. Your money talks!

Think about the advertising the clothing companies use to sell their fashions. How are women and men portrayed? Are they selling clothing with half-naked models? If companies choose to use their advertising dollars depicting women as objects, consider spending your money at other stores that do not. It is your responsibility as a consumer to use your cash in a manner fitting your dignity.

Choosing the Right Clothing for You

There's nothing more unattractive than a woman wearing what's trendy but looks terrible on her body type. This is fashion rule number one: If it's not attractive on your body, leave it in the store! There are so many women out there wearing low-riding pants that have a slight pouch of a stomach and would look much better in a pant that is cut a bit higher. Wearing the correct style for your body type will shave off at least ten pounds. Let's get one thing straight, though, all bodies are made in the image and likeness of God. You are beautiful. We live in a culture where the outward appearance is most valued. Since we have to exist in this culture, it's good to know how you can look your best.

There are several different body types that fit most women's shapes. Each has separate styles that flatter her shape. Check out the chart that follows and see if you can identify yourself. Then, read the fashion advice for your type.

The proper fit of garments is essential to looking your best. Here are a few tips on fit. Anything tight, especially across the bust or butt, will create a focal point and take attention off your face. It's too tight if there's wrinkling or pulling, if the garment appears to be painted on your body, or if there's pulling or gaping by the buttons. Wearing clothing too tight or too big adds pounds to the figure – not only that, too-tight pants can help develop yeast infections and who needs that just for the sake of fashion?!

If you wear your clothing too large, it appears sloppy. It's too big if the garment hangs off the shoulders, the clothing appears to sag or if another person could fit in it with you. Clothing should skim the body and reveal feminine curves without exaggerating them. Buttons and other closures should lay flat without puckering. The correct fit of clothing accentuates the body in a modest and appropriate way and slims the figure.

Always remember:

Focal point is simply, where the focus is. It is the first place the eye is attracted. It is said that the eyes are the windows to the soul, and the soul is what animates the body. This is where you want others' attention to be when they are looking at you.

Body Types

There are several basic body types that most women fall into. In our culture the most sought after type is the hourglass where the top and bottom are in proportion. This is what we see in magazines, movies, TV and other print media. However, this is not the norm for most women.

There are tips and tricks to "fake" the hourglass figure that many fashion consultants and stylists use when helping women. As a daughter of God, though, you must realize that whatever body type you have, it is beautiful to God. There was a time when all art and paintings were done of women who were neither hourglass in shape nor firm in tone so the world's definition of beauty always changes.

Not only that, what the culture thinks is attractive really isn't what God sees as attractive. After all, God sees your heart and it is your heart that has a special beauty. It may sound trite but it is so true that it has to be said again and definitely needs to be said here...

It is much more important
to be beautiful on the inside
than on the outside.

That being said, it is still good to look your best. To balance your figure, check the table below and see if you are making the most of your body type by the clothing you choose to wear.

Body Types

Triangle A	Triangle B	Inverted Triangle
A small waist, hips wider than shoulders, small bust	*Full waist, hips wider than shoulders, small bust*	*Shoulders wider than hips, average to large bust*

Round	Rectangle	Hourglass
Balanced hips and shoulders, Generous bust and waist	*Balanced hips and shoulders, undefined waist, average bust.*	*Balanced hips and shoulders, defined waist, generous bust*

Shape	Problem	Solution
Triangle	Hips wider than shoulders	-Add weight to your top with small shoulder pads -Nautical, square or yoke collar -Horizontal prints on top
Inverted Triangle	Shoulders wider than hips, average bust	-Add weight to the bottom -Fitted tops, flouncy skirts -Pants with pleats
Round	Balanced hips and shoulders, generous bust and weight	-Streamline with vertical stripes -Slenderize with dark solids -Keep focal point on the face
Rectangular	Balanced hips and shoulders, undefined waist	-Fitted long jackets with peplum -Diagonal lines and V-neck tops

Check out the following fashion tips to build a wardrobe and flatter the body.

Monochromatic Dressing (M.D.)

1. M.D. is the safest and most painless way to look thinner.
2. M.D. is the favorite trick of virtually every fashion designer. Why? Because it makes everybody look slimmer and taller instantly. Plus, it's always elegant and it's an extremely easy way to dress. Almost a total no-brainer!
3. Technically, dressing M.D. is wearing darks with darks, and lights with lights. It's wearing one color from head to toe. It works for two reasons:
   a) Color is the first thing most people notice about an outfit. Even someone who is clueless about fashion and rarely notices what anybody is wearing will notice color.
   b) Dressing in one color produces a strong, unbroken vertical line that elongates the body.

Cheating with Monochromatic Dressing: It's always fun and you can get away with it. Just keep your dark colors with dark, and your light colors with light.

♥ One color on the inside – top and bottom with a different color on the outside (i.e. a jacket).

♥ One color on the outside – jacket and bottom, with a different color top.

♥ Blend different shades of the same color.

♥ Add prints only after you have your basic 8-piece wardrobe. Buy only small prints and only small horizontal stripes if they are very close together and similar in color value.

♥ Add accessories – scarves, jewelry – to pull it all together. This will also draw the attention to the face.

♥ Use texture to add interest.

The good thing about fashion today is that there are so many choices in styles and colors, it is fairly easy to find flattering things to wear. Always buy the best quality of garments you can afford.

Some fun information about fabrics...

Natural Fabrics

➤ Cotton - Comes from the cotton plant. It is cool, comfortable and easy to clean. Examples include t-shirt material and denim. It wrinkles and shrinks easily.

➤ Linen - Made from the flax plant. It is cool, comfortable and can be hand washed or dry-cleaned. Jackets and skirts are made from linen as a spring fabric. It is known for wrinkling.

➤ Wool - Comes form animals such as sheep, goats and llamas. It is a warm fiber and is made into sweaters, jackets, skirts and pants. It can be hand washed or dry-cleaned depending on the garment. Some people find it to feel itchy on their skin. It should be stored with lavender, moth balls or in a cedar closet to keep moths from eating holes in garments made of wool.

➤ Silk - Made by silk worms. It is the strongest fiber. Blouses, scarves, dresses, jackets, skirts and pants can be made from it. It can be quite expensive. Some silk can be hand washed but most garments should be dry cleaned.

Synthetic Fabrics

➤ Spandex - A very stretchy manmade fiber that is woven with other fibers to make garments that are comfortable and gives "move-ability" to them.

➤ Rayon - A soft manmade fiber that is used for skirts, blouses and dresses. It is comfortable but wrinkles easily. It should be dry-cleaned. It is known to shrink when washed, even by hand.

➤ Polyester - Is a very versatile manmade fiber, which can be woven with any fiber to make the garment more comfortable and easier to launder.

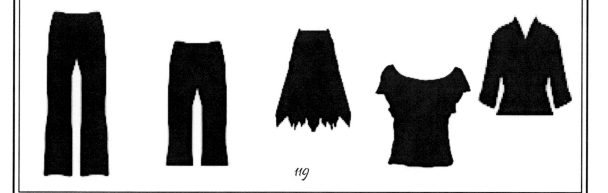

Some fun information about articles of clothing...

Skirts
- A line - fitted at the waist and hips with a flare at the bottom.
- Pencil - fitted at the waist and hips and narrows at the knees.
- Gored - fitted at the waist and hips with fullness past the knees.
- Straight - fitted at the waist and hips.
- Peasant - fitted at the waist with soft, flowing bottom.

Pants
- Capri - Short pants cut above the ankle
- Straight Leg - A cut of pants that fall straight from the hip.
- Pencil Leg - A fitted leg that narrows at the ankle.
- Flared Leg - The pant leg fits in the hips and thighs and widens at the ankle.
- Leggings - Form fitting leg coverings made of stretch fabric and hug the leg.

All About Tops

Types of Sleeves:
- Dolman - A long sleeve that is very wide at the top and narrow at the wrist.
- Set in - A sleeve, long or short that is sewn into the armhole of the top.
- Raglan - A sleeve that extends from the neckline and in, not "set in."
- Cap - A very short sleeve not going past the armpit.

Types of Collars:
- Notched - The type of collar seen on suit jackets, resembling a pair or wings with a triangle cut out of it.
- Shawl - A rounded collar on a V-neckline.
- Mandarin - A small standup collar and open in the front.

Types of Necklines:
- Jewel neckline - Also called a T-shirt neckline is a circular shape around the neck.
- Scoop neckline - A U shaped neckline.
- Boat neckline - A neckline which is two lines going across the collar bone.
- V necklines - Two lines starting at shoulder and meeting on the chest and shaped like a V.
- Square necklines – Are shaped like a square around the neck.

What two colors do I want to concentrate on?

1.
2.

What do I need to finish my 8-piece wardrobe?

Color _____

Color _____

_____ Jacket, Vest or Cardigan

_____ Jacket, Vest or Cardigan

_____ Top

_____ Top

_____ Pant

_____ Pant

_____ Skirt

_____ Skirt

What pieces do I have to mix and match?

_____

_____

_____

What pieces do I need to purchase in order to mix and match?

_____

_____

_____

What accessories do I want to add?

_____

_____

A Word About Undergarments and Other Private Things

If you haven't already done so, it's a good idea to get measured and fitted for a bra. Many department stores do this as a service to their customers. If you are not comfortable with having someone fit you, see the chart and directions below to fit yourself. Be sure you line up the tape measure correctly around your back to get an accurate measurement. By wearing the correct size and style of bra, you will give your "foundation a lift" and appear fit.

How to Fit a Bra

1. Measure all the way around just above your breasts for band size (i.e., 36 inches equals a size 36 bra).
2. For cup size, measure across the fullest part of your breasts. Then subtract the band size from that number.
3. Use this chart to find your cup size:

AA	½"
A	1"
B	2"
C	3"
D	4"
DD or E	5"
F	6"
G	7"

When choosing a bra, purchase the type that is comfortable. Here are a few tips on finding the correct fit for you:

➤ The back of the bra should lay flat and straight. If it rides up, it is too small around.

➤ If the cups wrinkle, they are too big and you should go down a cup size.

➤ If you have cleavage showing, the cup size is too small and you should go up one-cup size.

➤ If your breasts are showing underneath, the straps are "hiked up" too far and need to be let down.

Shape Wear

If you have a pouch in front, you may want to wear a panty that has a bit of spandex and comes to your natural waist. It's popular to wear fun and bright colored panties when you are young. However, when you wear more formal clothing, it's good to select the proper underpants. This will keep you from having panty lines or bumps in your clothing and your clothing will fit and drape better. If you would like to smooth your hips and bottom there are a lot of choices for shape wear. These used to be called girdles and were made of material similar to rubber. Can you imagine how those poor women must have sweat? We are lucky to find shape wear in comfortable materials.

In the 1950s women were much more conscious of modesty; girdles were worn as a form of modesty. The clothing at that time was fitted to reveal the feminine figure. The girdle kept ladies' bottoms from wiggling or jiggling. Have you ever sat behind a woman who did not have on proper undergarments and her bottom jiggled? Yep, that's distracting to guys and girls alike. So keep your wiggle nice and tight by choosing the right underpants.

A word about thongs and such: a lot of young women like to wear them because they don't show panty lines.

However, they don't do a thing about the wiggle or jiggle. Also consider that they are not "healthy" for you. The little string that holds the thong together can bring unwanted bacteria into the vaginal area, which can cause yeast and other infections. Bacteria thrive in warm, moist places. When you wear a panty with a cotton crotch, it absorbs moisture and pulls it away from the vagina. If you've been experiencing infections in this area and you wear a thong, you may want to choose an alternative panty. Wearing feminine undergarments makes you feel pretty and, in today's market, you can find both function and beauty.

While we're on the subject of personal things, think about bathing suits. Many women shave in order that pubic hair doesn't show when wearing a swimsuit. One thing to be aware of though is that it's not a good idea to remove all the pubic hair. Pubic hair protects the vaginal area from bacteria. It collects moisture and pulls it away from the vagina. If you remove it all, there will be nothing to keep this sensitive area from getting infections

Thoughts About Swimsuits

It is very popular today for young women to wear bikinis in the summer, whether in public to the beach or to a

friend's backyard pool. Our culture is so used to this that many girls don't even think about modesty when choosing a bathing suit. But, as a young Catholic girl, you should consider this: Our Lady carried Jesus in her womb and because of this she is called the Ark of the Covenant.  The womb area of a woman is sacred because it is there that she carries life. So, even though it is popular, it is never really appropriate to reveal the midriff. Ponder this the next time you go to purchase a bathing suit. At the very least, keep a cover-up near so that you can veil yourself when you are walking around.

Dress for the Occasion

Years ago, women really had a sense of style. Things were much more formal regarding etiquette and fashion. There were certain things that were worn at home such as slacks, jeans, housedresses, Capri pants or Bermuda shorts. These items were not usually worn in public except for occasions such as picnics; but, even then, dresses were preferred. Women wore hats and gloves in public and to Church. In fact, at Church women always covered their heads with a hat, scarf or mantilla. Dresses, suits and skirts were worn outside of the home.

What a change from today's culture, right? Now it's anything goes. You see athletic wear, shorts and t-shirts worn to picnics, the beach, to Mass and out for dinner. But is this really okay?

It is part of etiquette and good manners to dress appropriately for the occasion. It is a sign of respect, charity and kindness when you dress appropriately. Besides, dressing up is a lot of fun! Remember when you were little and you used to play "dress-up?" Well, now is your time for the real thing!

Enjoy being a "grown up" when it comes to maturely understanding that different occasions require different clothes. Set the example for your friends and even your family – if need be.

Look over the following examples for suggestions on how you may make some changes.

Picnics, Beach, Cookouts, the Movies:

- T-shirt
- Jeans
- Capris
- Shorts
- Flip-flops or tennis shoes

Casual Dining

- Jeans or pants without stains or holes
- Blouse, sweater, jacket, fitted t-shirt
- Accessories, jewelry, sandals or leather shoes or boots
- Skirts
- Dresses

Holy Mass

- Slacks – clean and pressed
- Skirts and jackets – ditto
- Dresses – ditto
- Accessories – ones that accentuate the face and don't draw attention to themselves
- Dress shoes or clean, fashionable boots – avoid any heel height that is difficult to walk in

Avoid these things always:

- Pajamas or boxers outside your home
- Sweatpants are for the gym
- Bra straps sticking out from under tops
- Halters and tops that look like lingerie
- Very short miniskirts and shorts
- Extremely low-riding pants or jeans
- Plunging necklines

It's fun to dress up. Fashion is fun. Be the trendsetter and dress appropriately for all the occasions in your life. Fashion is a way of self-expression. You can reveal a lot about yourself by your choices in clothing. Most girls have a certain style they always wear. Take the fashion personality test and see what category you prefer. You may find you like a combination of styles.

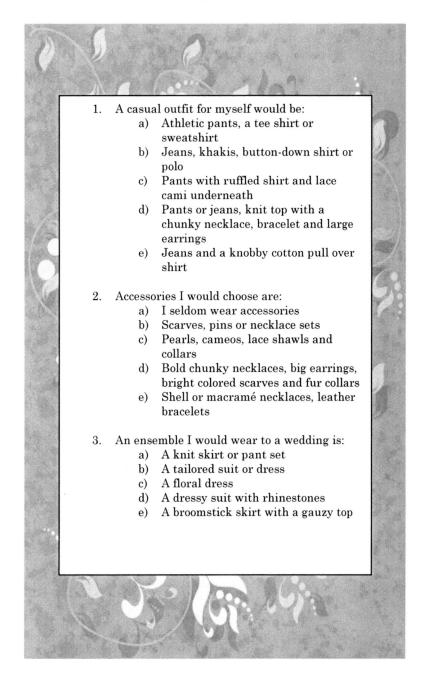

1. A casual outfit for myself would be:
   a) Athletic pants, a tee shirt or sweatshirt
   b) Jeans, khakis, button-down shirt or polo
   c) Pants with ruffled shirt and lace cami underneath
   d) Pants or jeans, knit top with a chunky necklace, bracelet and large earrings
   e) Jeans and a knobby cotton pull over shirt

2. Accessories I would choose are:
   a) I seldom wear accessories
   b) Scarves, pins or necklace sets
   c) Pearls, cameos, lace shawls and collars
   d) Bold chunky necklaces, big earrings, bright colored scarves and fur collars
   e) Shell or macramé necklaces, leather bracelets

3. An ensemble I would wear to a wedding is:
   a) A knit skirt or pant set
   b) A tailored suit or dress
   c) A floral dress
   d) A dressy suit with rhinestones
   e) A broomstick skirt with a gauzy top

4. My favorite type of shoes are:
    a) Tennis shoes or slides
    b) Loafers or traditional pump
    c) Ballet slipper or a pump with a bow on the toe
    d) The hottest new thing out there
    e) Birkenstocks

5. My favorite fabric pattern would be:
    a) Solids or stripes
    b) Solids, plaids, herring bone or tweed
    c) Flora or lace
    d) Animal print, geometric
    e) No real patterns, but soft natural textures

6. My favorite top would be:
    a) Tee shirt or sweatshirt
    b) Button-down blouse or polo
    c) Ruffled blouse
    d) Black knit with fur trim at the neck and sleeves
    e) Denim shirt

Mostly As: You are a sporty gal! You are most comfortable in athletic wear and tennis shoes. You don't like to dress up or wear accessories. Your main goal is comfort.

Mostly Bs: You are a classic young woman. You love the styles that change very little. Button-down shirts, blazers and basic skirts in timeless black, navy and red are your favorites. You dress these pieces up or down for the occasion.

Mostly Cs: You are a romantic at heart. You love to look and feel feminine. You choose lace and florals and feel pretty in them. Long, flowing skirts are a favorite.

Mostly Ds: You have a dramatic flair! You love attention and you wear things others are afraid of. You love being on the cutting edge of fashion. Your wardrobe is full of basic black, bold accessories and wild prints.

Mostly Es: You love a natural look and feel. You are happy with natural fibers, cotton, linen and wool. Sometimes your style resembles a free-spirit look. You take your cue from nature.

Skin,
Makeup
and Hair

Good to know...

Part of looking your best is taking care of your skin and, if you choose, wearing makeup. Many girls don't learn how to take care of their skin but still wear makeup. Basic skin care, though, should be the priority. When a girl is in her teens, she may experience excess oil and breakouts on her face, neck, chest and back. It is best to cleanse the skin at least once in the morning and once before bed with a mild water-soluble cleanser followed by a lightweight moisturizer with sunscreen for daytime and an appropriate lightweight moisturizer for bedtime. Toners are optional because they can be too harsh for some skin types. Change your pillowcase often and use a new washcloth each time you cleanse. If at some point you feel you cannot keep the blemishes under control, you may want to try going to a salon where they do facials or to a family doctor. Some teens will be prescribed a mild antibiotic to help with the breakouts. (On occasion girls may find that they are sensitive to antibiotics and develop a yeast infection. If this happens it is important to tell mom.) There are those that will experience more serious acne and will need to seek the help of a dermatologist with their parents. All of these things are normal for girls in their teens.

The skin is your body's largest organ! Take care of it well.

As a survivor of acne, I have to say it was no fun and caused me angst many times. I remember getting ready to go out with my friends to a football game. I was around sixteen at the time. I tried everything to cover all the millions of zits and no matter what I did all I could see was a mass of red bumps. I felt like my face looked like a pizza and spent more than a few tears that evening before finally going out.

Not long after that, my mother took me to the doctor. These are the times when a girl truly appreciates mom!

It's important to realize that even if you do struggle with acne, most girls pass through the acne stage without too many skin problems as adults. When talking about image-related things, remember that appearance is a minor part of who you are as a person. You must go deeper when image-related issues bother you. You do this by positive self-talk and prayer, which come from knowing that you are truly a daughter of the King. You must battle your bad thoughts with good thoughts because no one can do this for you.

If you choose to wear makeup, always apply it to clean skin and make sure to remove it every night before bed. Having a professional makeup artist or salesperson help you is a good thing so that you can try before you buy. Always purchase the best quality products you can afford.

Avoid heavy black eye liner. This type of application really makes a girl look harsh instead of young and beautiful. If you use foundation, choose a color that is the same shade as your face – you want to avoid the "mask" look. Gently apply makeup. Pulling or tugging the skin stretches it out.

Tweezing the brows will bring attention to your eyes and make them appear open and bright. Be careful not to remove too much of the brow or you will create an "unusual" look. It's best to follow the natural arch and remove only the "straggler" hairs. Many women have found out the hard way that brows don't always grow back.

The skin ages, sags and wrinkles as you get older, but you can slow down the aging process by using a product with at least a SPF 15 and wearing a hat when in the sun. Exposing your skin to the sun continually or excessively may cause premature aging and the possibility of skin cancer. It's hard not to get a tan when you are young but you really should think of the long-term consequences.

Look into self-tanning lotions, spray tans or bronzing powders as options for a healthy glow.

It seems when you are young, that you will always be young; but, youth does fade. However, developing good skin care habits while you are young will last a lifetime.

and always remember...
While you take care of your physical appearance, building up your inner self to be a true reflection of who you are, a daughter of the King, is critical to your joy and happiness!

BASIC SKINCARE

The skin is the largest organ of the body. It is the only organ that can be "regulated." This means, that by changing products or habits, it will act differently. The skin keeps the organs and muscles protected from the outside world. Breakouts and rashes are impurities being purged from the inside.

During the teen years, hormones are changing and producing more oil. This can cause blemishes or blackheads. Besides caring for the skin, there are a few other things that can be done to keep breakouts under control:
- Shower and shampoo frequently
- Change pillowcase daily (if this makes a lot of wash for mom, offer to help with laundry)
- Use clean towels and washcloths (if this makes a lot of wash for mom, offer to help with laundry)
- Limit or avoid greasy foods
- Limit or avoid sugar and white flour intake
- Limit or avoid dairy intake
- Increase vegetable and fruit intake
- Drink lots of water to help the skin eliminate impurities

There are five steps in
taking care of skin

STEP 1:
CLEANSE THE FACE

Use a gentle and water soluble cleanser. The worst thing to use is soap and water. This will dry out the skin and send a signal to the oil glands to produce more oil. Many teenagers feel their skin is not clean unless it feels tight or tingly. This is a myth. Most soaps not only dry the skin but have ingredients that clog pores. Use upward and outward motions to clean your face. You can use a soft washcloth with cleanser on it, or your fingers. Rinse with cool water after cleansing.

STEP 2:
EXFOLIATING

This step will remove dead skin particles that can clog pores. In doing this the newer, healthier skin surfaces. A topical, mechanical scrub is best if it is extremely fine. Over-scrubbing can break open blemishes or cause abrasions. It is important to be gentle when using a scrub. Again, use upward and outward motions with either your fingers or cloth. Avoid the eye area. Rinse clean with cool water. Those with acne should not use a scrub. The other option for exfoliating is Alpha Hydroxy or Beta Hydroxy, both are mild chemicals that slough the skin without using a scrub. They are available in many skin-care product lines.

STEP 3:
TONE

Use a toner to make the skin feel clean and smooth. Benzoyl peroxide is considered the best over-the-counter drug to use in fighting blemishes. If you do not have blemishes, do not use a toner. Toners can dry the skin if they are not needed.

STEP 4 & 5:
MOISTURIZE AND PROTECT

Everyone needs to moisturize the skin, even if you have oily skin. A light moisturizer will help regulate the oil production. Protect the skin by using a product with SPF 15 or greater. By staying out of the sun, the skin will be less damaged and look younger longer. Foundation is part of the protection step. There are a variety of foundation types to choose from such as cream foundation, cream-to-powder, mineral powder and liquid.

Basic
Makeup
Application
Tips

Basic Makeup Application Tips

Step 1: Concealer

- ♥ Use to cover blemishes, dark circles or other flaws
- ♥ Choose a color at least two shades lighter than your skin
- ♥ Use a sponge applicator and dab on skin and do not pull or tug the skin

Step 2: Foundation

- ♥ Choose a foundation that is the same shade as your skin color
- ♥ Use a foundation with at least SPF 15
- ♥ Choose foundation to go with your skin type (ex: oil free, cream to powder or liquid)
- ♥ Use a sponge applicator and dab makeup in spots all over face and eye lids
- ♥ Blend in gently in an outward motion
- ♥ Don't apply under the chin or on the neck

Step 3: Powder

- ♥ Use a large natural hair brush to apply loose or pressed powder
- ♥ Tap brush on the edge of the container to knock off the excess
- ♥ Apply in a downward motion

Step 4: Eye Makeup

- ♥ There are many techniques to use with different eye shapes. The following application works for all shapes
- ♥ Use natural hair eye shadow brush
- ♥ Knock excess powder
- ♥ Apply lightest shadow from brow to lashes
- ♥ Select a darker shade in the same color family and apply to the crease and eyelid
- ♥ Use a dark brown, charcoal or black to line the upper lash line only; if you line lower, it will close in the eye
- ♥ Apply mascara from bottom of lashes to the top; discard mascara after 6-12 weeks to avoid eye infections

Step 5: Eyebrow Arch

- ♥ Follow the natural arch of the brow
- ♥ Fill in the brow with a natural brown eye shadow that matches the color of your brow – shadow is a softer look than a pencil
- ♥ The end of the brow should end at the corner of the eye
- ♥ Tweeze or wax stray brows for a clean look; do not make them too thin; stay with the natural arch

Step 6: Blush

- ♥ Blush is applied to give contour to the face – not for "rosy cheeks"
- ♥ Use a natural hair brush if using a powder and knock off excess
- ♥ If using a cream or liquid, use your fingers or a sponge, apply a couple dots and blend from end of nose at the outside corner of the eye, underneath the cheek bone, near the hair line, toward the ear
- ♥ Apply powder the same way

Step 7: Lipstick and Lip Liner

- ♥ Always use a lip liner and use short, feathery strokes to outline the lips
- ♥ Choose a liner in the same color family as the lipstick
- ♥ Fill in with lip liner and go over with lipstick
- ♥ Using a lip brush will make your application cleaner
- ♥ Add gloss

Hair

When you are trying to look your best, hair plays a big part in the overall look. To find a flattering or attractive hairstyle, it's advantageous to find a good stylist. The best way to do that is to get a referral from someone whose hair you really like. Hairdressers come in all varieties but in most cases, you get what you pay for. There are plenty of great stylists who start out working at discount salons and move to more upscale salons. A good stylist should always take time to have a consultation with you before she does anything to your hair.

The hairdresser should be knowledgeable about face shape, color, cutting, including a variety of cutting techniques and products to help you maintain your style.

This is the time to learn to love and accept how God has made you so your whole life can be filled with the joy that comes from that knowledge.

As a hairstylist, I highly recommend using professional quality hair products such as shampoo, conditioner and styling aids. You will find that they perform better and do not put a waxy buildup on your hair.

As with all image-related topics, remember to choose styles and colors that are right for your unique face and body. Don't go with the trend if it isn't just right for you. I once had a client with a prominent nose. She was young and insisted on wearing her hair long and straight. Unfortunately, that choice of hairstyle drew attention right to her nose. As she matured, she asked my opinion on her hairstyle. I suggested a layered cut with a soft spiral perm. What a difference this made in her appearance. The focus was off her nose and on her eyes! The new haircut softened her entire look.

No matter what the style is, and how cool it is on others, if it doesn't flatter you, avoid it!

There are many things for a girl to pay attention to when it comes to looking good. Beauty is something that our culture emphasizes. Though a girl must take care to always look her best, it is important not to get carried away. It is not good to spend large amounts of time in front of the mirror. Young women have to work at finding a balance so as not to become self-centered. Always remember that everyone has God-given beauty. Realizing this is important because it helps you to overcome the culture's view of beauty and recognize God's view of beauty and dignity.

Embrace your uniqueness.
You are a princess, a daughter of the King and are worth more than a rare jewel!

Before you try to decide what hairstyle is best for you, make sure you are taking good care of your hair. It is important to shampoo your hair every day to avoid that greasy look, if you find that it needs it. The best kind of shampoo is a clarifying shampoo followed by a light conditioner. Clarifying means a shampoo that deep cleans and gets rid of buildup of products like mousse or gel or hairspray. Even if you don't use products like that, a clarifying shampoo really deep cleans. If you highlight or color-treat your hair, use a shampoo specifically for color-treated hair. Your stylist can recommend the right product for you.

It is highly recommended that you use a salon shampoo and conditioner. It costs a little more, but you don't have to use much and it lasts a long time. In a family, there is only so much money to spend on all their needs. Shampoo and conditioner from the salon may seem like a luxury. Deciding priorities is an important part of maturing and talking with your mom about these  things is a part of that process. Together you and your mom can determine priorities for your beauty regimen. You can help make those priorities happen by saving your money and doing without an extra pair of jeans or your weekend gourmet cup of coffee – you get the idea. Let your mom see that you care about yourself *and* about the family. There are many beauty supply stores where you can find large quantities of salon shampoo and conditioner which tend to run a bit cheaper because of the size.

Anyhow, five liters of salon shampoo lasts about a year for a family of five. Use about a dime size or so every time you shampoo your hair. Use conditioner the same way. Professional shampoo may not lather up but not to worry, it is working! Professional products don't build up on the hair like drugstore shampoos do. This is what causes hair to look greasy by noon, even if you showered and shampooed your hair that very morning.

Check it out: take a sharp scissors and carefully scrape the blade over a small chunk of hair in a slow, upward motion. If you have been using inexpensive shampoo and conditioner, you will see a white buildup on the blade. This is balsam. It' like candle wax and is an ingredient in nonprofessional products. Once you begin using quality hair products you will notice a difference in how your hair feels and how it styles.

Do you like to swim? Make sure you shampoo after each swim. Chlorine can build up in the hair and ruin your beautiful locks. If your hair is full of chlorine, it will appear very shiny and sometimes have a touch of green to the color. When wet, it will feel like cooked spaghetti. You can do a clarifying treatment at the salon or at home to help strip the chlorine. Purchase the clarifying product, shampoo hair, apply product, cover hair with a plastic bag and let it sit for 15-30 minutes. Rinse and apply a light conditioner. Don't forget the conditioner or your hair will be a total rat's nest! The clarifier opens the hair shaft and pulls out the impurities, leaving the strand open, which causes tangles.

When combing out long hair, start at the part line and work in small sections, combing down. This will keep your hair from breaking. (Ever hear your hair snap, crackle and pop? It's hair breakage.) Combing this way will result in nice smooth hair.

Dandruff is something girls may or may not experience. Dandruff refers to a flaky scalp. It may be caused by several things. First, the scalp may be dry which will cause flakes and itching. Secondly, the scalp may be oily and the flakes may be large oily flakes. Next, shampoo and other products may not be rinsed out and this causes flakes of products, not the skin. Whatever the cause, the best way to be rid of dandruff is to use a coal tar shampoo every day until you get the problem under control. Then you may go back to using the clarifying shampoo. Coal tar shampoo can be found in a pharmacy. It doesn't smell very good, but, boy it works!

Girls often make the mistake of copying movie stars or fashion models when picking a hairstyle. Why is this a mistake? Well, you are unique. You have different hair and features than the famous people seen on TV, in magazines, or in the movies. Their stylists work hard to find the best hair design just for them. Problem is, girls mimic these styles, even if these styles look awful on them or just aren't right.

Here are some things to consider when deciding which style is just right for you:

-FACE SHAPE-
If you are unsure what your face shape is, pull back your hair and look in the mirror. You can also ask your hairstylist to help you decide which shape you have.

-FACIAL FEATURES-
With your hair pulled back, decide what is your best feature – for example, your eyes or your smile. You will want to emphasize this. Always accentuate the positive.

-LIFE STYLE-
Think about how much you will really work with your hair. How active are you in sports? Do you like wearing hair accessories such as barrettes? It's not a good idea to have a style with lots of layers if you won't style it or you play on a sports team and need to keep your hair out of your face. It just won't work.

-HAIR TYPE-
Is your hair thick or thin? Straight or curly? Do you have cowlicks that make your hair hard to style? If you have curly hair, you will not be able to wear a straight, flat-layered style. Learn early that it's best to work with the hair you have, not fight against it.

-TIME-
How much time do you plan to spend on your hair? Are you willing to get up early before school to blow dry and style it?

-COST-
How often will you need a trim to keep the style? How much money are you willing to spend to keep up your hairstyle? What are the family priorities? Again, the family has expenses for all the members. You may have to choose between keeping up your hair or a new pair of shoes. It's not all about you, but about learning how to pick and choose what it most important. You may have to make an arrangement with mom that you pay for some things with your hard-earned money.

CONSIDER ALL OF THESE THINGS
WHEN CHOOSING A HAIRSTYLE
BUT **ALWAYS** REMEMBER
THAT AS A DAUGHTER OF THE KING,
HOW YOU TREAT PEOPLE
AND WHAT IS INSIDE
IS **MUCH MORE IMPORTANT!**

There are a number of styling aids on the market today. Just like shampoo and conditioner, it is best to use the professional brands from a salon or a beauty supply store. Many inexpensive brands flake, buildup, or dry out the hair. Remember, a little dab will do ya!

The hair industry, like fashion, is constantly changing and you will see new products all the time. However, below is a list of basic styling products. Choose what is right for you.

✝ Mousse: Used to give body and fullness
- ♥ Squirt about the size of a quarter into your hand and rub your palms together.
- ♥ After the foam is like a lotion, apply to the wet hair shaft.

✝ Gel: Gives holding power
- ♥ Apply gel the size of a dime or nickel into your hand and rub the palms together.
- ♥ Apply the gel to the wet hair shaft closest to the scalp and pull through.

✝ Thermal spray: Helps when styling with heat, like a curling iron or blow dryer
- ♥ Can be used on wet or dry hair.

✝ Pomade: Helps to define a dry style by separating pieces of hair.
- ♥ Apply a very small amount to the palms and pull through the hair shaft.
- ♥ Use fingers to "piece out" your hairstyle.

✝ Hair sprays:
- ♥ Aerosol: Comes in a can and sprays a mist. It varies in holding power from a working hold to a "cement hold."
- ♥ Non-aerosol: Comes in a bottle with a spray top. Varies in holding power but comes out in a wet mist.

✝ Curls:
- ♥ There are many products for curly hair to help straighten or smooth. Always ask your hairdresser for the newest options.

	Face Shape	Try	Avoid
	Oval Gently rounded hairline with a slightly narrower jaw than temples	-Short, medium or long hairstyles -Textured layers or bangs -This shape is balanced and can wear a variety of styles	-Heavy bangs and forward-styled hair because it covers the face and can add weight
	Triangular Dominant jaw line and narrow cheekbones and temples	-Shorter, fuller hair at the top and narrowing at the jaw -Off-center parts -Wedges and shags are good -Tuck hair behind the ears	-Long, full hairstyles that draw attention to the full jaw line -Center parts -Long straight hair, no bangs
	Round Full face, round chin and hairline with widest point at the cheeks	-Styles with fullness and height at the crown and front -Off center parts -Short hairstyles styled off the face -Medium lengths past the chin -Layered top -Close to the face cuts	-Chin-length cuts -Center parts -Very short hair -Fullness at the cheekbone
	Square Strong jaw line, square hairline	-Short and medium cuts -Loose curls and waves around the face -Wispy bangs, razored sides to soften face -Height at the crown -Angle cut bobbed cuts with razored edges, above the jaw line	-Long straight styles -Straight, boxy bangs -Straight cut bob
	Heart Wide temples and hairline with a small chin	-Weighted cut at the chin, like a bob -Side-swept bangs -Soft-razored bangs or none at all -Flipped up shag with longer layers on the top	-Short full styles, height at the crown -Top heavy styles

The Catholic Church teaches that you are an amazing, unique created human being loved by your Creator and on earth for a reason. JPII's inspiring document *Mulieris Dignitatem* expresses this fact in the very opening paragraph, which ends with these profound words meant to dwell within your heart and give you hope and understanding of who you are in Christ....

That is why, at this moment when the human race is undergoing so deep a transformation, women imbued with a spirit of the Gospel can do so much to aid humanity in not falling.

John Paul II's Mulieris Dignitatem

Inspiring words for you to live by from beloved Pope Benedict XVI...

Love – caritas – is an extraordinary force which leads people to opt for courageous and generous engagement in the field of justice and peace. It is a force that has its origin in God, Eternal Love and Absolute Truth. Each person finds his good by adherence for him, in order to realize it fully: in this plan, he finds his truth, and through adherence to this truth he becomes free (cf. Jn 8:22).

Encyclical letter "Caritas in Veritate"
Supreme Pontiff Benedict XVI
2009

Financial
Responsibility

Throughout your teen years you should be discerning God's call upon your life. You may be going to college, you may be getting married, or you may be a single woman. Regardless of how you are called, you will be called to financial and fiscal responsibility. This simply translates in understanding how to live within your means and make the most of your time.

Like all the things we've discussed in the book, there's no better time than the present to begin to put good things into action. You are developing a prayer life, you are behaving in a way fitting the daughter of a King, and you ought to be financially responsible with your allowance or the money you are earning at a job. There are many ways to go about this – and you should always rely on mom and dad for guidance – but here are a few things for you to keep in mind as you grow into a beautiful woman ready to serve God.

According to Webster, the word "BUDGET" has a number of definitions but the one most associated with it is as follows:

a) A statement of the financial position of an administration for a definite period of time based on estimates of expenditures during the period and proposals for financing them;

b) A plan for the coordination of resources and expenditures;

c) The amount of money that is available for, required for, or assigned to a particular purpose.

When I think of the word "BUDGET," I usually defer to definitions (b) and (c) above. At times, it is a bit scary to focus on that word as it seems to carry a negative connotation. I would like to propose a slightly different way of looking at this word, defining it, and making positive use of it. Below is my definition of "BUDGET."

B = Begin -- to become familiar with the expenses in your life;

U = Understand -- where your money is going;

D = Develop -- a plan;

G = God -- is in the center of all plans;

E = Execute -- the plan;

T = Tips & Triumph - you have successfully taken control of your finances!

So, "Let's start at the very beginning" as is said in the popular song from *The Sound of Music*. The beginning means tracking where your money is going - everyday. I suggest you start with a notebook. Put the date at the top of the page and write down every penny you spend that day. Whether you spend money via cash, check, charge or online, the most important thing is to write it down. Some of your expenses may be items that you purchase rarely or bills that come due only quarterly – like your car insurance. At this point, don't be concerned about that. Just track your expenses everyday for now. Here are some examples:

Monday

Beauty products $25.00

Lunch at school $6.00

Sue's birthday gift $18.00

<u>Tuesday</u>

Dad's birthday $22.00

<u>Wednesday</u>

Car insurance $375.00

Once you have started this procedure, you have *begun* -- B has been accomplished.

You should track your expense throughout a full month or two to really get a feel for where your money goes. If your mom or dad feels that you waste money, this can give you an idea if you really do and help you to stop!

Tracking your expenses is an ongoing procedure that can really benefit you so you want to continue doing that and keep yourself aware of how you spend your money.

Now, let's talk about the letter U - understanding where your money is going. In order to do this, I'd like you to take another piece of notebook paper. On this page, I would like you to write your take-home income at the top and then list the major categories of your expenses broken into two groups. Listed below are some category suggestions; however, as this is your budget, use the categories that best suit your needs. There may be more or less than the ones listed below, but I would just suggest that you do not have more than about a dozen.

<u>Income</u>

Monthly Income

<u>Expenses - make sure to determine a monthly figure</u>

Car insurance; Car payment; Church donations or other organizations you support; Home expenses – this is a nice time to consider "paying" a few bucks in rent to mom and dad every month even if they just put it into an account for your future

College – if you are discerning a college career, you should be putting aside a few dollars each month for those expenses; Clothes; Gasoline; Food; Entertainment – movies, books, video games etc.

Once you have created this list, start adding up your expenses and put the total next to the categories you have created. For example, look at your spending sheet, add up all the times you have eaten out, and put the total on the category line "Eating out." Expenses like your car insurance only occur once in a while, so just enter the amount across from that category.

I found this exercise difficult. Being honest about "wants" and "needs" is challenging. But understanding where your money is going is the only way to take control of your finances. Please continue tracking your daily expenses.

Years ago I heard a speaker who changed my life. Mary Hunt spoke about her experiences with money and incredible debt ($100,000), which prompted her to write the book *Debt-Proof Living,* which we've included in our own book suggestion list in this book.

Her advice was simple and basic and while really applied to adults more than teens, it is worthwhile to know ahead of time to avoid problems! She said to get rid of all but one credit card - and stop charging! I, obviously, did not have a plan at that point in time. I used my credit card every time a car repair needed to be done or my kids needed clothes. Even though I was a wise shopper, those expenses continued to add up, as did my charge account interest. There was no way I could pay off my balance each month. I didn't use my credit cards to buy a fur coat, but I also didn't have a reasonable plan of how to manage them.

Mary Hunt suggested writing a spending plan. This spending plan, of course, could not exceed my income so I needed to think through carefully those "needs" and "wants." One of her wisest suggestions was to have a "Contingency Fund." Others have called this an "Emergency Fund" or "Rainy Day Fund." The bottom line is that we all need money that has been put away for emergencies - then we don't lose control of where our funds are going.

What might that be for a teenager? Maybe it is money put aside for unforeseen car repairs or even, at your age, to be able to pay for three months worth of "expenses" if you lose your summer or part-time job. The teen years are great prep years to be a responsible, joyful Catholic woman and nothing robs us of joy as does debt.

One important part of your Contingency Fund is that you don't take money out of it unless it is a dire "emergency."

We've talked about tracking expenses, developing a spending plan, having a safety net, and getting rid of credit card debt – or more accurately for you, never acquiring it.

We now need to talk about the letters "G," "E," and "T" because **G**od is part of all plans and it is time to **E**xecute your plan for financial responsibility and experience **T**riumph with our tips!

You may be wondering why I have references to Mary Hunt. There are a multitude of other financial gurus out there, but the one characteristic that I felt set her apart was that she was a Christian who practiced her faith. As important as all the particulars are in taking control of your finances, having God at the center of your plans takes precedence. I suggest giving 10 percent to God, whether it is in a weekly contribution to your parish, Right to Life, missionary appeals, Diocesan collections, or any other choices you may have to help others. There are many needs in the church so choose what is important to you.

Tithing isn't just for adults! Tithing is for any Christian who is earning money and is an excellent way to honor God with the fruits of your labor. It may not be easy to get in the habit but remember that diligence and perseverance are key traits that are valued in Scripture. No matter what, the point is to make an effort to live responsibly and know that God is always at the center of what you do.

Since we all have many expenses, putting aside 10 percent may not be easy. However, there are endless ways to cut back. No matter what you do, pray about it and ask God for advice. He will surely guide you.

Here are a couple of suggestions of ways in which you can keep more of your money and have more to give God:

✞ Learn some great recipes that are both yummy and inexpensive to make – we've included some at the end of this section and bet mom will love the help and ideas!

✞ Check out the gardening section of this book to grow your own plants and give as gifts.

✞ The next time you get invited to a friend's birthday bash, consider making her a beautiful gift basket filled with things you've made – face it, that's both cost effective and shows that you really do care about her. See our bath salts recipe at the end of this section as just one item that you may include in your gift basket.

✞ There are some excellent clothing buys at thrift stores – don't be embarrassed – check them out!

✞ See if your mom would agree to a clothes swap set up at your house and get some of your friends together who want to "swap" clothes – this gives you new things to wear while not costing a dime – just make sure the swaps are fair.

✞ Spend a day at the spa at home – do your own manicure and pedicures – great stress relief and a wonderful way to connect with mom so consider inviting her.

Being financially responsible also means using your dollars wisely from another perspective. We live in a world where "money talks" and you want to make sure that you spend yours in stores or on products that don't ultimately support abortion or other things that are against the Catholic Church. There are many Catholic resources for finding out the real Truth behind such organizations. A great place to start is by checking out the Susan B. Anthony organization. They are committed to helping and supporting pro-life causes.

LEAN ON ME, DEAR ONE

Lean on me, for I care about you.

Let My strength support you, My love carry you.

I'm here for you.

Lean on Me, and I'll help you through any pain.

I'll be your eyes when you feel you have to turn away.

I'll be your ears when you can't bear to hear what has to be said.

I'll be your heart, always filled with courage and hope.

Lean on Me and trust in Me.

You know I'll be there for you, through thick and thin,

in the best of times and in the most challenging of times.

I am your rock, your fortress, your everything.

Lean on Me and discover complete serenity.

You are My child, and I will never forsake you.

Lean on Me, for I am always with you

as your indwelling Christ.

Love your friend, Jesus

Recipes to please any budget...

Sloppy Joes

6 lbs. hamburger (ground beef, ground turkey); Minced onions; 2 Tablespoons regular mustard; ¼ cup brown sugar; Worcester sauce; Salt; Pepper; Ketchup

Add onions to skillet and preheat, add meat and chop as it is browning. When the meat is thoroughly cooked, add brown sugar and Worcester sauce (as with the other ingredients, this is to your taste), salt, pepper, and lots of ketchup. The amount of ketchup is determined by how thick or sloppy you like your mix. Then place the sloppy joes in a crockpot on low and let them simmer for several hours.

No-Fail Swiss Chicken

6-8 boneless, skinless chicken breasts; Italian seasoning; Kraft Swiss cheese; Cream of chicken soup; Pepperidge Farms Herb Crumb Stuffing (not cubes); ½ - ¾ stick butter

Grease 9 x 13 pan; Lay chicken flat; Top with Italian seasoning; Add Kraft cheese slices. In small bowl, mix cream of chicken soup with ½ can of water. Stir and spoon over cheese slices. (These steps can be done the night before or in the morning, cover, and put in the refrigerator until ready to bake.)

Melt butter and stir in with 2 cups of herb stuffing; Sprinkle over chicken. Bake uncovered 1 hour in 350 degree oven (or until chicken is cooked through). **Alternatives:** Chicken tenders can be substituted for chicken breasts; Cheddar cheese can be substituted for Swiss cheese; With the chicken soup, mix ½ cup of white wine or milk instead of water; Before the herb stuffing, broccoli bits can be added as well as drained water chestnuts. Enjoy!

Apple Crisp

Arrange 2 cups raw apples, pared and diced, in a greased 8" x 8" baking pan. Sprinkle as desired with cinnamon. Mix: 1 cup flour, 1 unbeaten egg, 1 tsp. baking powder, 1 cup sugar and ½ tsp. salt.

Stir with a spoon into coarse crumbs. Sprinkle over apples and pour over all 1/3 cup melted butter. Bake 30 minutes at 350 degrees. (Optional: Serve with a scoop of vanilla ice cream.)

Manicures and pedicures that won't break the bank!

Materials needed:

- ♥ Containers to soak feet
- ♥ Bowls to soak hands
- ♥ Towels to dry feet and hands
- ♥ Cuticle remover
- ♥ Nail polish remover
- ♥ A pusher
- ♥ Nippers
- ♥ Emery boards
- ♥ Mild, disinfectant soap
- ♥ Pedi-file
- ♥ Exfoliator
- ♥ Polish
- ♥ Decals
- ♥ Mini-polishes with tiny brushes to make designs (Sally's Beauty Supply)

Manicure Steps at Home

Step 1: Soak hands in warm, mild soapy water.

Step 2: Apply cuticle remover and pushback and trim cuticles with nippers.

Step 3: Shape the nail with a nail file. To remove length, use a coarser file.

Step 4: Apply base coat

Step 5: Apply polish. Always polish in three strokes, starting in the center and then each side.

Step 6: Apply topcoat

Step 7: Clean up around the cuticle if needed.

Pedicure Steps at Home

Step 1: Soak feet in warm, soapy water.

Step 2: Apply exfoliating lotion and massage in.

Step 3: Use pedi-file to remove dead skin.

Step 4: Rinse feet.

Step 5: Apply cuticle remover; push back and trim cuticles.

Step 6: Clip toenails giving the nails a square shape. File if necessary.

Step 7: Apply emollient lotion.

Step 8: Apply nail polish remover to the toenails to remove lotion.

Step 9: Apply base coat.

Step 10: Apply polish.

Step 11: Apply topcoat.

Step 12: Remove excess polish with remover.

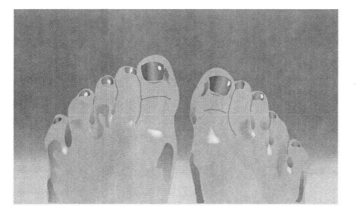

Daily routines
do not need to
break the bank
or take up all
your spare time.

Learning how to
budget both –
money and time
– will help you
become more disciplined.

Being part of the culture today does not mean being self-absorbed but being self-aware. Taking care of your appearance is an outward sign of knowing your worth as a person and embracing the fact that you are a princess.

Make These Yourself

Bath Salts

Try these salts when you need a little TLC and relax in your own private spa! These make great gifts too.

Ingredients and Directions:
Epsom salt
Essential oils, such as lavender, or orange
Food Coloring

Mix 1 cup of Epsom salt, ¼ cup sea salt, add 2-3 drops of essential oils, and food coloring to your preference. Add to bath water and enjoy!

Put the colored salt in jars. Decorate the jars with lace, sequences, or beads and give as a gift.

Skincare

Pore Strips This mixture will clean your pores (clogged pores can cause blackheads or pimples).

Ingredients and
Directions:
1 Tablespoon of
plain unsweetened
gelatin (look in the
isle where Jello is
sold) and 1 ½
Tablespoon of milk

Mix the two
ingredients in a
bowl. Heat until it
forms a paste. Apply the mixture to parts of the face such

as nose, chin, or forehead where blackheads and pimples appear. Let dry. Remove and look. You will see how much "yuck" was in your pores!

Sunburn Relief Ingredients and Directions:
1 small grated potato (peeled); 2-3 teaspoons of flour; water

Mix the ingredients, adding enough flour and water to make it the consistency of cake batter. Spread over the burned area. Leave on the face for 20-30 minutes. Rinse with water.

Lip Exfoliant (for Dry, Flaky Lips) Ingredients and Directions:
Ingredients; Sugar; Olive Oil

Mix equal parts of the above ingredients. Apply to the lips rubbing gently back and forth. This will remove dry skin leaving your lips soft and moisturized. Rinse with water.

And a word about time...we've spent a lot of "time" talking about money but time is something you should also be keenly aware of as it is as valuable as money, if not more valuable!

The same sorts of principles that apply to money also apply to time. So, if you feel like you can't get a handle on all the demands of your time, track what you do just like you did with money. Apply the same principals of including God and making Him a top priority. All these things will help you grow into a thoughtful, God-fearing woman whose priorities are right placed and whose life will be lived just as He intended!

How Does
Your
Garden
Grow?

Many girls today play sports and do all sorts of things that keep them busy, healthy and active. Along with such things as playing basketball or soccer, girls should realize that there are good, old-fashioned hobbies that are worth their time and effort as well.

One such hobby is gardening! There's often nothing like getting out in the sun – of course wearing sunscreen or a very lady-like wide-brimmed straw hat – and digging into the soil. God intended us to be connected to the earth in a special way and gardening does just that. Imagine the beauty and peace in planting a "Mary Garden" or in discovering the amazing way that a garden is God's pharmacy!

I planted the seed .... but God made it grow. This means that neither he who plants nor he who waters is of any special account, only God gives growth.

1 Corinthians 3:6-7

This verse from the Bible is talking about spiritual growth, but it also fits into the growing of our gardens. No matter how carefully we scatter the seeds or plant our flowers and vegetables, it will be a gift from God that brings our work to fruit.

If you don't know much about plants or how to care for them, whether inside or out, here is some valuable information that is meant to inspire you or at least pique your interest in all things green!

Basic Plant Information

The main parts of a plant are: roots, stems, leaves, and flowers. Each of these parts works together like a miniature factory where the plant growth is orchestrated in a pre-designed system influenced by its surroundings.

Roots are the underground foundation of a plant. They anchor the plant and absorb water and minerals from the soil which then travels to all other parts of the plant. The water and minerals travel through tubes made of xylem cells and phloem cells. Xylem cells carry the nutrients up from the soil, and phloem cells carry nutrients from the leaves through the stems and down to the roots. Having well-prepared and fertilized soil will help the root system work more efficiently.

The stem is that part of a plant that connects its roots and leaves. It is the plant's main support system above the ground. Fibers and thick walls give the stem its strength. The transport system made up of the xylem and phloem cells carry the nutrients through the stem. This transport system needs a sufficient amount of water to function well. Usually we can depend on the rain to take care of this, but occasionally we may need to do our part with a little extra watering.

A leaf, which is a plant part that grows out of the stem, is the food-making part of the plant. Through a process called photosynthesis, leaves manufacture food for the plant. This process takes place in the middle, spongy layer of cells when the light from the sun joins carbon dioxide and water together. This process produces a form of sugar called glucose. The top and bottom layers protect the leaf and keep it from drying out. The bottom layer also allows the exchange of gases needed in food making. A leaf contains veins that allow for the transport of water and manufactured food. This is just a brief description of the functions of a leaf. It would take many pages to give a detailed account of the working of a leaf.

The flower is the reproductive part of a flowering plant. The main parts of a flower are the stalk, the petals, the pistil and stamen. All flowers have the same basic parts, even though each variety looks very different. It is inside the flower that seeds are produced. Fruits form around the plant seeds as a protection. Some fruits, such as plums and cherries, have only one seed. Others, such as tomatoes and apples, have a number of seeds.

Each part of the plant carries out an essential job needed in the life of the plant. God, a very thorough and astute engineer, has constructed these four parts into a compact and efficient product which we call a plant. I cannot imagine what the world would be like without plant life. Plants are so important to all of us! They are our main food source. They purify the air, give shelter to animals and birds, give us wood products for homes and everyday activities, bring a great deal of beauty to the world and so much more.

Next time that you are planting a flower or digging up a plant, take time to look it over carefully. Examine the different parts of your plant. Enjoy the beautiful gifts that our Creator has generously given us in the plant world!

And God said, "Let the earth put forth vegetation,

plants yielding seed, and fruit trees bearing fruit

Genesis 1:11

Green, growing, living things – even the most seemingly unattractive plants – have their own type of beauty. Look at the thistle. Its prickly stalks can be vicious if you brush up against them with your bare arm, and farmers cringe when they see this invasive plant taking root in their fields; however, anyone who is lucky enough to slowly drive by a group of thistle in bloom is awed by their feathery purple flowers glistening in the sunlight, paying beautiful tribute to their Creator. What treasured gifts God has given to mankind to use for which to be good stewards!

Consider the lilies of the field...even Solomon in all his glory was not arrayed like one of these. Matthew 6:28

Lilies are the favorite flowers of many people because of their beauty and first hint of spring.

Perennials are plants that bloom year in and year out – they bloom "perennially" versus annuals which have to be planted, you guessed it, annually. Daylilies are versatile, attractive, easy-to-care-for perennials. Hardy, pest-resistant and quick to multiply, they make a beautiful addition to a garden. Daylilies are a good background behind shorter flowers; making a sweeping scene of mid-summer color. Massed together in a group they showcase an area with their color. Used along a slope, they become a carefree ground cover.

Although daylilies tolerate some neglect and a variety of soil, they respond better with care. They prefer decent soil and sufficient moisture, becoming more drought-tolerant after they have become established. Light mulch will help soils retain moisture. Soil rich in organic matter encourages blooming. A little fertilizing is good, but avoid mixes with high nitrogen content. Most daylilies like full sun, but some, such as pastel colors, grow well in shade.

Remove spent blooms. Your lilies will look best with a little grooming throughout the season. Although each flower only lasts a day, blooms continue to open over a long period. Monitor plants for spider mites and spray if needed. In the fall, the old foliage may be removed by cutting back to the ground. Although in a country-like setting this may not be necessary – they will probably do fine.

Daylilies should be divided every 3 to 5 years. This chore can be made easy by using two spading forks held back-to-back, pushed into the ground at the desired spot, and then pried apart. Lift out an entire clump and separate into fans (a group of leaves with roots attached). Have the soil in the new location workable. Some tips on planting the lilies are: loosen soil about one foot below ground level, remove a little soil, leaving a upside-down cone shape slightly below ground level, spread the roots of the lily over the cone and cover with soil; water well after replanting.

Daylilies are one of the most popular perennials. They come in a multitude of colors and price ranges. You can buy a fan for just a few dollars or find a friend who will give you a start.

A Mary Garden

It is a Catholic tradition to acknowledge and honor the unselfish and holy life of the Blessed Virgin Mary. One way of doing that is to plant a *Mary Garden*.

In the Middle Ages, missionaries and travelers spread stories across Europe about flowers named after Mary and various times of her life. *Mary Gardens* that featured these flowers became popular there, and later the tradition made its way to America. Around 1932 it is believed that the first *Mary Garden* in the United States was constructed on the grounds of St. Joseph's Church in the Woods on Cape Cod.

Now, many flowers that symbolize the name of Mary grace gardens throughout this country. If you, too, would like to honor our Blessed Mother through flowers, perhaps you would like to create your own special garden spot that showcases plants that carry her name. The center focus of the garden is a statue of Our Blessed Lady. The size of the garden does not matter. In fact, people with limited space can use a small area and a few select flowers to surround their statue. If you are an apartment dweller, you can set up your *Marian Garden* in a window box or even use a small statue with a single flowering plant. Reflecting on Marian flowers can be a perfect starting point for meditating on the life of Christ through Mary.

To help set up a *Marian Garden,* flowers and their meanings are listed below. This list is far from complete but should give you enough information to begin.

1. *Lily:* Legend tells us that the Angel Gabriel held a lily in his hands when he came to tell Mary that she was chosen to be the mother of the Savior. Lilies are often depicted in pictures of Mary as an indication of purity and grace.

2. **Columbine:** This flower is often called Our Lady's Slipper. Legend says that this flower sprang from the earth where Mary's feet stepped when she was on her way to visit Elizabeth.

3. **Rose:** The rose symbolizes Mary as the Queen of Heaven. The red rose represents sorrow. The white rose shows joy, and the yellow rose stands for the honor bestowed upon Mary.

4. **Violet:** The violet is a symbol of modesty and simplicity; humble acceptance to the words from the angel Gabriel...."Let it be done unto me according to Your will."

5. **Carnation:** Legend says that the carnation bloomed on the night of Jesus' birth; a sign of Mary's joy at the Child's birth.

6. **Oxeye Daisy:** It is said that when the wise men reached Bethlehem they looked for a further sign to guide them to the new king. King Melchior saw a white and gold flower and knew which building to enter.

7. **Star of Bethlehem:** The shape of the flower is said to resemble the star that the Magi followed to find the Christ Child.

8. **Snowdrop:** The snowdrop is said to have bloomed in February when Mary took Jesus to the temple to present him to God.

9. **Rosemary:** It is believed that Mary hung the linens of the Holy Child on the rosemary bush to dry. Afterwards, the bush carried a sweet aroma.

10. **Forget-me-not:** The tiny blue flowers of this plant represent Mary's eyes.

11. **Meadow Cress:** This plant is called Our Lady's Smock. It stands for the fine linens made by Mary's hands. It is said that Mary learned to weave as a young girl.

12. *Lavender* This fragrant plant represents purity, cleanliness and virtue – Mary's spotlessness and chastity.

13. *Marigold:* Early Christians placed marigolds around statues of Mary in place of coins calling them Mary's gold.

14. *Bluebells:* These bell-shaped flowers resemble tiny thimbles and represent Our Lady's working hands. They were often called Our Lady's Thimbles.

15. *Speedwell:* This plant is also known as Mary's Resting Place. A legend tells that its blossoms marked each spot where the Blessed Mother rested during the flight into Egypt.

16. *Lily of the Valley:* Lily of the Valley is called Our Lady's Tears. It is said that her tears fell at the foot of the cross and turned into tiny fragrant blossoms.

17. *Iris:* The Iris is a flower, like the Lily, that represents the Annunciation.

18. *Herbs:* Almost any herb can be used in your garden to represent Mary. Soothing and healing herbs represent her heavenly love and mercy. Bitter or sour herbs represent her sorrows and sweet smelling herbs reflect Mary's spiritual sweetness.

19. *Fuchsia:* These gently drooping flowers resemble pendant earrings. It is said that the child Jesus playfully hung these flower 'jewels' on his mother's ears.

20. *Fleur-de-Lis:* This is sometimes called the Ave Maria flower. There is a legend that tells of a fourteenth century knight. He was extremely wealthy but renounced his worldly possessions and entered a Cistercian Order of monks. He was very devout but not terribly smart. He could never remember more than the first two words of the Ave Maria prayer even though a teacher gave him numerous lessons. Since he loved Our Lady very much, he would continually repeat the first two words of the prayer, day and night: *Ave Maria, Ave Maria.* Some of the monks ridiculed him for his simplicity and

told him that Mary would not listen to his unfinished prayer. He grew old and when he died, he was buried in the chapel yard of the monastery. As proof that Mary heard and loved his short but earnest prayer, a fleur-de-lis plant sprang up on his grave. On every flower shone in golden letter the words, *Ave Maria*. The other monks finally realized his great devotion for the Blessed Mother; and her devotion to him.

God's Pharmacy

"I have food to eat of which you do not know." Jn 4:32

A Sacrament is an outward sign instituted by Christ to give grace. The seven Sacraments are visible actions that the Church performs for all of us to witness. They are gifts from Christ; they give us grace to fortify our spiritual health. God is pretty smart – okay He's way smart – and it makes sense that He may have instituted ways to supplement our physical health. Here are just a few interesting, thought-provoking examples:

It has long been said that eating **carrots** will help improve eye sight. Scientists believe that vitamins and nutrients in carrots help enhance blood flow to the eyes. If you look at a carrot slice, you will notice that the circular designs look like the pupil and iris just like a human eye. That is interesting!

A **tomato** has four chambers and is red; just like a heart. Tomatoes contain lycopine that helps purify and feed the heart.

Grapes hang in a cluster that has the shape of a heart. Each grape looks like a blood cell. Research shows that grapes are great heart and blood food.

If you crack open a walnut shell, you see that the meat of the **walnut** looks like a little brain; a left and right hemisphere and an upper and lower cerebellum. It is believed that properties of walnuts help develop neural-transmitters for improved brain function.

Oranges and other citrus fruits look like the mammary glands and actually assist the health of the breasts and the movement of lymph in the breasts.

Diabetics may be interested in the fact that **sweet potatoes** balance the glycemic index. Notice the shape of the sweet potato; it looks like the pancreas.

Kidney beans, which are shaped like the human kidney, actually heal and help maintain kidney functions.

Bone strength is replenished when you eat **celery** or **rhubarb** because of the sodium content supplied by these vegetables. Celery and rhubarb look like bones.

Onions look like the body's cells. Scientists believe that onions clear waste material from the body cells.

These visual clues may just be a coincidence. However, we all know that God is a master at details and that there are probably many indicators for living well that He has left us. We just need to take time to observe and appreciate the treasures that are around us.

"Stand still and consider the wondrous works of God." Job 37:14

Starting Your Plants Indoors

"Train up a child in the way he should go, and when he is old he will not depart from it." Pro 22:6

Interestingly, there are great similarities between growing plants and raising children. Both of them need nourishment and the right environment to mature properly. If we want our plants to be strong and to grow tall in order to reach their leafy arms skyward, we must provide them with an adequate beginning. Even more so, we need to make sure that the roots of our children are planted firmly in their faith by covering them in a Christian environment. If we provide a daily, Christ-like example as soil, fertilize it with prayers (the Rosary is an excellent nutrient), and water it with the Sacraments (be sure to obtain Baptismal water for new starts), our children – you! – will grow strong in the love of Christ and daily lift their arms heavenward in praise.

Many people like to use seeds to start their garden plants indoors. This can be an enjoyable project and can save on the purchase of potted plants from the store, since the cost of seeds is much less than the cost of a plant. Because of the small cost of most seeds, you may decide to experiment with raising a large variety of plants. Do keep in mind, though, that some seeds are not suited for indoor starts or simply do better by being planted directly in the garden --nasturtiums, sunflowers and wildflowers are examples of such flowers.

The cost of the seeds can vary greatly, depending on the kind of seed. Seeds for a rare plant will command a much higher price than most "common" seeds but will still be less than the cost of buying a specialty plant. So why not grow a few rare gems on your own! Enjoy the challenge and the rewards of such an endeavor.

In addition, recognized name brands may demand a higher price. The packaging is usually showier, but most "off brands" are just as good. The percentage of germination is governed by law.

How do you find the information needed for starting your seeds indoors? Simple! Just check the directions on the back of the seed packet. The directions on the back of the package should tell you everything that you need to know about how to grow the seeds. They should list information on when, where (shade or sun), how deep, the time it takes for germination and spacing information.

Starting and growing seeds indoors is easy and fun. All you need is soil (potting soil or a plain soil with sand and vermiculite added), a container (store purchased flats and pots or home containers such as egg or cottage cheese containers), a warm, bright spot, moisture and the seeds.

After you have your seeds, prepare your container; make sure it has drainage. Also, make sure the container(s) are clean. You don't want to start off with mold or bacteria in the container that could contaminate your seeds.

Add your soil. You can use garden soil. However, I would sterilize garden soil because it could contain insects or disease. You can do this by baking it in the oven at 175 degrees for two hours. It is much easier to purchase a good quality planting or starting mix.

Next, plant the seeds at the proper depth. Check the back of the package for this information. Then, spray or sprinkle water over the soil to moisten it; don't use a strong spay or it will wash the seeds to the side. Keep the soil moist until you see the young sprouts begin to emerge. Then water as needed.

At this time, the container should be moved to a place where the new plants will get bright light. Southern sunlight would be best if it is available. If you do not have the sunlight, use grow lights or fluorescent tubes. Keep the light about 4 inches above the seedlings as they grow. Try to give the plants about 12 hours of light, but don't leave the lights on continuously. Turn the container occasionally, or the plants may grow lopsided as they reach for the light. The temperature should be between 65 and 70 degrees for starting seeds.

When the young plants reach about two inches high, they can be transplanted into individual pots or spaced out in a container. Lift the seedling with a spoon under the root ball. Don't lift by the stem because you may crush it.

When your plants have reached the desired height and all chance of frost is past, move your plants outside. A week or two before planting outdoors, begin "hardening" your plants by moving them outside for a short period of time. Then, leave them out for an increasingly longer time each day. If you make the transition to the outdoors too sudden, the plants may wilt or even die. When the plants are ready, it is best to transplant them on a cloudy day or late afternoon when the sun is not at its peak. Prepare the ground outside and water the ground and the seedlings before transplanting. This helps prevent shock. Dig a hole about twice the size of the root ball; set the plant into the hole so that the root ball will be covered completely. Press the soil firmly around the plant. Water again and every day the first week unless it rains. Then, water as needed. Happy planting!

Houseplants

As a young woman, there will be many things that you are beginning to learn to prepare you for the time when you are the "woman of the house" if marriage is the vocation to which you are called. Being the woman of the house has many responsibilities, including making your home warm and inviting for your husband and children. Houseplants are just one way to do that. Here is some valuable houseplant information that you may want to share with your mom or ask if you can be "in charge" of the houseplants now as you grow into a woman of the house.

"There is material enough in a single flower for the ornament of a score of cathedrals." John Ruskin

With a little care and attention, growing houseplants can be an easy and enjoyable experience. Always remember that even the easiest to grow and most resilient plant will need water, light, and sometimes new soil. Plants that grow inside need care just like outdoor plants do.

Before you bring home a new plant, scrutinize the conditions of the area where you want to keep it. Check the humidity, temperature, light level, potential drafts, and floor or shelf space. What type of plant will best survive in that area? Also, how much time do you have to devote to your plant? Many plants work well because they require infrequent watering and limited maintenance. Others, such as orchids, require special attention. Since your plant will share your home or office space, you will want to consider which of the many varieties of these "green friends" will best thrive in your surroundings.

After you have evaluated your environment, you are ready to select the types of plants that you would like. When you find a plant that you want to bring home, inspect it carefully to make sure it does not have signs of diseases or pests. Unfortunately, houseplants can suffer from diseases like bacteria or fungus. Look at the plant, including under the leaves, for signs of off-color spots or mold. Also, look for indications of pests. The most common kinds are aphids, mealy bugs and mites.

Most of these pests can be easily taken care of, if you've found them on any of your houseplants. Aphids, which are tiny bugs that live and feed in groups, can be removed by a blast of high-pressure water. Mealy bugs, a bug with a white, fluffy, wax coating, can be treated by using a little alcohol on a cotton ball. The alcohol will penetrate the wax and eventually kill the pests. Mites, a very small insect that can form a web over the plant (the affected leaves may appear spotted), can often be blasted off with water like aphids.

If you like to take your houseplants outside during the summer, be sure to inspect them before you bring them back into the house. It is possible for them to be exposed to pests and disease from your yard.

If your plant does not have any indication of pests or diseases but still seems to be having a problem, you may need to recheck your growing conditions. Yellowing leaves may be an indication that the plant has been sitting in water for extended periods of time. Leaves and flowers may begin to droop if soil remains too wet for too long, or if there is a dramatic change in temperature. Another possibility could be lack of oxygen. You may need to change the soil so that oxygen can better reach the roots

If your plant is spindly and weak looking, you may need to place it where it can get more sunlight. Be careful because extreme levels of sunlight may cause the plant to become discolored and yellow. For those who have small windows or a limited natural light, you may want to consider a "grow light." There are a variety of incandescent and fluorescent lights available at discount and hardware stores or on the Internet.

If the tips of the leaves are brown, you may be over fertilizing and "burning" the plant. Brown tips could also indicate that your plant is too dry or the temperature is too low.

If the plant does not seem to be growing well or is yellow or discolored without leaves falling off, you could have a root-bound plant. The roots may need more room. A fresh batch of potting soil can increase air circulation.

Plant Fertilizers and Repotting Your Plant

If you use a high quality potting soil, your house plant should have the organic nutrients it needs to grow properly. You may also choose to give your houseplants some fertilizer to encourage their growth. Slow release fertilizers are a good choice for houseplants. Many organic and natural fertilizers will help minimize the risk of burning your plants and are usually slow releasing. However, there are a number of good chemical fertilizers on the market, too.

Whether you decide to use an organic fertilizer or a chemical one, make sure that you read the instructions carefully. Applying too much can be harmful to your plant. Spring and summer are the best times to fertilize houseplants. Many plants are more dormant in the winter and need to rest. Also, it is important that you check the NPK number. This number lists the nutrient content of the fertilizer. You need to select the nutrient combination that is best for your plant.

Nutrient values (NPK) are expressed as total percentage of weight as packaged. N stands for the nitrogen. Nitrogen is responsible for the vegetative growth of the plants above ground. P stands for the Phosphorus. *Every single plant bears the imprint of the Lord* Phosphorus is essential for healthy growth of roots, fruit and flower development and disease resistance. K stands for the Potassium. Potassium is essential for the development of a strong plant.

Houseplant nutrients is sometimes called 'plant food'. It is sold in a variety of forms; granular, crystalline, liquid, or tablet. The label should tell you the NPK ratio. Some plants can be fertilized every two to three weeks, but most will not need additional fertilizer for several months.

If your plant has sufficient light, water, fertilizer, and appropriate temperature conditions but does not seem to be growing well, it may need more space for its roots. If your plant is "root-bound," the roots have filled up the pot and no longer have sufficient room. Other indications that the plant is root bound are when the water runs out of the bottom of the plant quickly, or the plant needs more frequent watering. It is time to repot your houseplant with a larger container and new soil. A general houseplant potting soil is fine for most plants. However, it is best to check and see if you have a plant that prefers a specific soil mixture (such as orchids or cacti). For most plants, it is recommended to use a potting soil which contains both vermiculite and perlite.

When you have your new container and soil ready, gently pull up the root bound plant and shake off the soil. You may need to gently work some of the roots apart if your plant is extremely root bound. Next, add new soil to the bottom of the new pot and place the plant into the pot. Add more new soil around the root ball. Do not pack the soil too tightly. It is not necessary to fill the pot all the way to the top with soil, but make sure that the roots are well covered. Then, water thoroughly.

Now that we have discussed caring for your house plant, let's talk about some of the types of plants from which to choose.

One of the most popular and easiest to grow is the *Philodendron* plant. Philodendrons can grow as climbers or non-climbers and are great for hanging baskets. They have a lovely heart shaped leaf and are an easy maintenance plant. They like moist soils and should be kept out of full sun. But don't leave them in standing water and do let them dry out a little between watering.

Another favorite is the *Snake Plant* which is also called *Mother-in-Law's Tongue.* This plant can grow rather tall (four to five feet). It prefers filtered light but can handle some direct sunlight. Be careful not to over water this plant, especially during the winter months. This could cause the roots and stems to rot. The Mother-in-Law's Tongue has an attractive stiff leaf, often with a nice stripe design.

Jade Plants like bright light. However, be careful if you move the jade. A sudden change from filtered light to bright light can cause sunburn. Jades are usually easy to grow. You can let them dry out somewhat in the winter, but water frequently in spring and summer. A Jade plant can even bloom (usually in the winter) if the amount of light they receive is to their liking.

For a low maintenance plant try the **Cast Iron Plant**. It can go for long periods of time without watering (about eight to ten days). This plant does well in low light areas and tolerates varying temperatures.

The **Corn Plant** grows well in full or filtered sunlight. It does not need a lot of water or fertilizer. If you can get it to bloom, it has a pleasant smelling flower.

Golden Pothos, also called **Devil's Ivy**, is easy to grow. Keep it out of full sun and do not over water. This would be a good plant in a low-lighted area in your home or office. You can easily grow new starts from cuttings of this plant.

It is always nice to try to keep an **Aloe** in the house. The Aloe likes high levels of sunlight. Soak it well when you water it and then let it dry out before the next watering. The juice of the Aloe is known for its soothing effect on small burns. It gives almost instant relief.

African Violets have a bit of a reputation for being difficult to grow. Those who have success have a perfect window to place them in. They are a beautiful plant and are worth the effort it may take to have them in the house. African Violets need indirect sunlight and moist soil. You can lightly water every other day, but avoid letting the plant stand in water.

One of the best hanging houseplants is the **Spider Plant**. It seldom has problems with pests or disease, and you can let it dry out between watering. The long, striped leaves give a nice effect when they cascade down the side of the planter. It likes partial shade or partial sun. It is easy to get a start from the Spider plant because it produces shoots, often called runners, which can be set in soil to begin a new plant.

German Ivy is another good choice for a hanging basket. It grows up and over a pot in a trellis like form. Water the ivy well and then let it dry out a bit before the next watering. The German Ivy prefers filtered light.

Begonias produce a pretty, delicate flower. They like medium to low level light and moist soil. My grandmother always had begonias and geraniums growing in a corner window above the sink.

Coleus is another attractive plant. It has multicolored leaves that can give a stunning effect in a grouping of houseplants. The Coleus grows well in bright-to-filtered light and prefers moist soil. Don't let it dry out for long periods of time.

Crotons can also add a bit of color to your house plant selection. They require full sun and frequent watering.

A popular plant with different colored flowers is the *Christmas Cactus.* The flower colors can vary from red, orange, white or pink. Keep it in a moderately sunny area and don't let it get dried out. Keep the soil moist but not saturated. To induce the plant to produce flowers you may need to provide cooler temperature and less light.

These are just a few of the more popular houseplants. You may also want to look up information on *Gardenias, Geraniums* and *Maidenhair Fern*.

May Jesus, Mary and Joseph be our guides in the garden of life.

Friendships are
like gardens...
Having a
good variety is
beautiful
to behold!

Cemetery Planting

The Corporal and Spiritual Works of Mercy are ways in which we take care of other people and honor Jesus. Here is a list:

Corporal Works of Mercy

Feed the Hungry

Give Drink to the Thirsty

Clothe the Naked

Welcome the Stranger

Visit the Sick and Imprisoned

Bury the Dead

Spiritual Works of Mercy

Counsel the Doubtful

Instruct the Ignorant

Admonish the Sinner

Comfort the Sorrowful

Bear Wrongs Patiently

Pray for the Living and the Dead

Using your gardening interest can be a way of performing either of the works of mercy. Taking care of a grave is a blessed way to bury or pray for the dead. The gardening act itself will bring you closer to the ways in which Jesus has asked us to do such things. If this is something you want to do, here are a few tips or guidelines to follow:

Some cemetery boards do allow annuals (flowers that grow only one season) and perennials (flowers that will return each year) to be planted. The general rule seems to be that the flowers may be planted directly above the headstone with a maximum planting area of 24 inches by 10 inches.

Some boards allow small shrubs or bushes in designated monument lots that consist of a certain number of combined lots (usually at least 8). It is the family's responsibility to keep the flowers watered and looking nice. Most cemeteries do a fall and spring clean-up. Some will even mulch around the plants at the end of summer. Again, check with your particular cemetery board and find out specific regulations.

While you mull over which plants would give an aesthetic view to a grave site and whose care would fit into your schedule, take a few minutes to consider something even more important: the spiritual care of your loved ones. Prayers and Mass requests for those who have passed away are equivalent to planting spiritual flowers.

Perhaps the love that we show by our prayers will be seen by God as a thing of beauty much like the ornamentation that we add to a grave site is seen as beautiful by those who stroll through the cemetery. And don't forget to keep your own soul adorned in grace and goodness; we don't know when God may call us away from our physical life. Spiritual maintenance will be well rewarded; the Lord said ...*eye has not seen, nor ear heard, nor the heart of man conceived what God has prepared for those who love Him.* 1 Corinthians 2:9

What would be some suitable plants for the grave site? A lot of it will depend on the family's tastes and whether the area is in shade or in sun. It would be good to look for something that is fairly hardy and requires low maintenance. You may also want to consider a color scheme.

Stick with a basic color or pick several colors that coordinate and compliment each other. Shorter flowers are often better (although a taller or spike-type flower in the center or at the back can give emphases if placed strategically). If you want the arrangement to change each season or each year, you should plant annuals. The choices are numerous.

A favorite annual for many people is the *Impatiens* flower. Impatiens come in a vast array of vibrant colors that make a very eye-catching display.

Choose some colorful "hardy" annuals or some perennials. Hardy annuals are flowers that are technically annual but will often come up year after year as long as the weather is not too severe. Violets, Pansies, Violas, Dianthus, Sweet Williams and Forget-me-nots are some flowers that many people like.

These are just a few choices from which to select. If your cemetery allows live planting, decide what you like, check the area conditions (shade, sun, dry, etc), the amount of space available, and the characteristics of the plants (height, hardiness, etc.). With these things in mind, have a restful time planting and praying!

Violets are hardy, fragrant flowers with a sweet heart-shaped leaf. They do not grow tall and like shade or partial sun.

Pansies, despite their name, are pretty hardy annuals. They can bloom throughout the entire spring. Pansies come in shades of red, white, blue, purple, yellow and orange. Some have "faces," others don't. They come in sizes that range from small (1" across) to large (4 ½" across).

Violas, from the violet family, are often considered miniature pansies, but they are actually perennials. They have color and markings that are similar to pansies. "*Johnny-jump-up*" violas are a good choice for small areas.

Dianthus are hardy annuals that come in white, pink, red, lavender and maroon. They are some of the longest *lasting and showiest of the spring flowers.*

Sweet Williams are a biannual type of dianthus. They are shorter and have smaller flowers.

Forget-me-nots produce clusters of tiny flowers. Their colors range from pale to deep blue and pink to white.

Portulaca, often called Moss Rose, is a beautiful ground hugging flower. You can plant these succulent type plants where it is hot and dry and still obtain beautiful blooms in red, orange, yellow, purple or pink.

Hostas are shade tolerant, lily-like plants. Their white, lavender or purple blooms form on an erect stem. Hostas usually prefer some shade.

Bleeding Hearts have dark green fern-like foliage. They are a perennial favorite with their tiny white or pink heart-shaped flowers.

Don't forget to check on regulations regarding grave blankets. This is usually a covering for a grave made from a pine tree and may or may not have decorative ornaments such as a ribbon on it. Grave blankets are usually placed upon graves during the winter months.

Consideration: Oftentimes graves are left unattended because close relatives are no longer in the area to take care of them or may be deceased themselves. If you are tending to your own relative's graves and see a grave that is in need of weeding or some gentle care, consider doing this yourself and offering it up to Christ.

Stations of the Cross

If you are looking for a beautiful way to meditate upon the Passion of Christ – as both a way to draw yourself nearer to Him and to pray for the Holy Souls of Purgatory – praying the Stations of the Cross is ideal.

An excellent resource for you is:

*Walk New:
A Way of the Cross for
Teens*

by Kathryn Mulderink and illustrated by Father Victor Kynam.

Every Life
Is a
Vocation

Every Life is a Vocation

Most teen-aged girls get a bit nervous when asked *Do you have a vocation?* They automatically think they are going to be recruited to a convent. They don't really understand what the word "vocation" means.

The word vocation means a call from God. Everybody, including YOU, has a call from God. The word vocation refers to three different things:

1. Christian vocation, which comes with Baptism, and it's a call to know, serve and love God in your life. All Christians have this calling.
2. Vocation also refers to a "state in life." It's a commitment to a particular Christian lifestyle such as the clergy, consecrated life, matrimony or single lay state.
3. Vocation means a personal relationship you have with Jesus. It is you, with all of your strengths and weaknesses, trying to know, love and serve God in a personal way through a personal commitment.

Pope John Paul II talked a lot about personal vocation during his papacy. It was one of the central themes of his teaching. God has created each person with gifts and talents oriented toward specific purposes and a way of life. It is up to each person to discern how God wants him or her to use these gifts in their profession, family life, Church and civic commitments for the sake of the greater good.

Planning vs. Discerning

There is a huge difference between discerning your vocation and planning your life. You see, when a person makes plans to become a teacher, fashion designer or dental hygienist, the focus of their planning is: What will make **ME** happy? What do **I** like to do?

When a person discerns a vocation, she asks herself bigger questions: What does **God** want from me? What will make **God** happy? What would **God** like to see me do? See the difference? People who plan but do not discern, organize their lives in order to reach personal satisfaction. This does not bring happiness. When you discern and you do what you think God wants from you, you will be happy!

But how does a person discern a vocation? Pope John Paul II explained in the Apostolic Exhortation *On the Vocation and Mission of the Lay Faithful* that it is a *"gradual process... one that happens day by day."* It involves lots of prayer and reflection on one's life, asking – begging – God to show you what it is that He wants from you.

The Vocation of Women: Mulieris Dignitatem

In 1988, John Paul II wrote an Apostolic Letter in which he reflects on the Dignity and Vocation of Women. Have you read it yet? This letter is a real treasure. The late Pope wrote that the dignity of woman is based on her being created in the image and likeness of God, therefore she is called to eternal union with God – the special vocation of women, collectively and individually, is to welcome and care for human life. Yes, you read correctly, every woman is called to be a mother, either in the physical or spiritual sense. Both signify a sincere gift of self. This is what the vocation of women is all about: *woman can only find herself by giving love to others* (Mulieris Dignitatem). God gave women special gifts such as a great sensitivity, intuitiveness, generosity and fidelity to fulfill this vocation.

Our Lady, the Blessed Mother, is the highest expression of the true dignity and vocation of woman. After the fall, domination took place of "being a sincere gift" and therefore living "for" the other: "he shall rule over you." The dignity of women went down the drain because of sin. Through history then, woman was dominated by man. At the Annunciation, when Mary gave her "fiat" or "yes," she restored the dignity of woman to it's original state: equal to man and made in the image and likeness of God. Mary's "fiat" allowed women once again to give freely of themselves.

As mentioned before, there are several vocations, that is, states in life, for women: consecrated life, matrimony and single.

Consecrated Life

God gives many women a vocation to consecrated life, which is a form of Christian living to follow Our Lord in a more intimate way. To do so, a person takes vows or other sacred bonds and commits herself to observe the evangelical counsels of chastity, poverty and obedience. Consecrated life comprises religious orders, consecrated hermits and consecrated widows among others. By far, the largest number of candidates for the Consecrated Life join community life through what are called religious orders in which they live a common rule under the leadership of a superior.

Religious Orders: Religious Life

Religious life was born in the east during the first centuries of Christianity. Lived within institutes canonically erected by the Church, it is distinguished from other forms of consecrated life by its liturgical character, public profession of the evangelical counsels, fraternal life led in common, and witness given to the union of Christ with the Church. (*CCC #925*)

There are several stages for a woman to enter religious life: admittance, postulancy, aspirancy and novitiate. During these periods, a person is able to reaffirm her vocation.

1. **Admittance and Postulancy:** This refers to the period of time from when a woman – a candidate – requests admission to a religious order until she enters the novitiate.

2. **Novitiate**: This refers to the period of training and discernment prior to taking vows. During this time, the novice is often dressed in special clothing which, while distinct from the secular dress, is not the full habit worn by professed members of that community. A novice spends her day praying, doing manual labor and receiving instruction about the religious life she is preparing to embrace. A novice is free to quit the novitiate at anytime if she was to discern that was not her true vocation.

3. **Profession:** By religious profession, the candidates make a public vow to observe the three evangelical counsels. Through the ministry of the Church they are consecrated to God, and are incorporated into the institute, with the rights and duties defined by law (Code of Canon Law, 1983). One of the effects of these vows is that the candidate is no longer free to marry and if she at some point would want to leave the order, she would have to seek a Papal Indult. When a woman does her profession, she receives her religious habit from the Superior of her community. Religious profession can be temporary or perpetual. Temporary profession may not be less than three years nor longer than six years and the candidate has to be at least 18 years old. Once the time has been completed, the candidate is asked if she wishes to renew or to do a perpetual profession, otherwise she is to leave the order.

Different Religious Communities do different kinds of work:

✝ Contemplative orders are cloistered, which means the sisters don't leave their convent. Their lives are devoted to praying and making sacrifices for the entire world. Examples of these are the Poor Clares, Carmelites and the Perpetual Adoration Nuns.

✝ Semi-contemplative orders do active work but usually don't leave their convents, except to work. They may teach or run orphanages. Examples of these are Assumptive Sisters, Dominican Sisters of Mary, Mother of the Eucharist and Dominican Sisters of St. Cecelia.

✝ Active Life Communities dedicate their lives to teaching, hospital works and mission work. They live and work outside a community house. Examples include Franciscan and Medical Missionaries of Mary.

Consecrated Virgins

From apostolic times Christian virgins and widows, called by the Lord to cling only to him with greater freedom of heart, body, and spirit, have decided with the Church's approval to live in the respective status of virginity or perpetual chastity "for the sake of the Kingdom of heaven" (CCC# 922).

A consecrated virgin is a woman living in the world or in a religious order, who dedicates herself to follow Christ more closely through a life of perpetual virginity. The diocesan Bishop consecrates her to God. Her commitment is to serve the Church by means of prayer, penance and apostolate, according to the spiritual gifts she has been given by her Creator.

Consecrated women can form themselves into associations to observe their commitment more faithfully (CCC# 924).

The one who has hope lives differently; the one who hopes has been granted the gift of new life.

Pope Benedict XVI 2008 Apostolic Journey to the United States

Matrimony

Many girls dream, from the time they are very little, to get married, have children and live happily ever after...just like in a fairy tale. Matrimony *is* a beautiful vocation to which a husband and a wife have been called by God from all

eternity. Their meeting, attraction to each other and decision to marry are not a result of blind chance, but are part of God's divine plan through which husband and wife spend their lives striving to get each other to heaven.

Matrimony is the Sacrament by which a baptized man and a baptized woman bind themselves for life in a lawful marriage. Jesus Christ instituted this Sacrament, although from the beginning of creation God had already established this intimate community of life and love. *God himself is the author of marriage* (CCC# 1603).

There are two essential properties to Matrimony, which cannot be separated from one another nor excluded from the conjugal bond:

1. Unity and Indissolubility

Nowadays, Hollywood has taken charge to discredit the real meaning of marriage. There are so few movies out there that portray a couple happily married, husband and wife committed and faithful to each other – the norm is divorced couples, people cheating on each other and people cohabitating. This is not what God intended! God created Eve from the body of Adam. This should be seen as beautiful proof of the equality and union that is intended to exist between husband and wife. Matrimony has always been a sacred contract, and as said before, Our Lord raised matrimony to the dignity of a Sacrament. When a man and a woman marry, they "are no longer two, but one flesh." God calls the spouses to grow in their unity through mutual self-giving.

...Until death do us part. Marriage is indissoluble, which means perpetually binding, or incapable of being dissolved. This is not something the Catholic Church invented, but is something ordained by God from the very beginning. Only the death of one of these spouses can dissolve the marriage bond. Do you know that there is no such a thing as divorce in the Catholic Church? Many people are shocked about this, because divorce is very prevalent in our times and many marriages end up in "divorce." Legally speaking, divorce is a separation of the spouses, giving them the "right" to marry again. But as said before, Christian marriage is indissoluble.

Martin and Rachel were married in the Catholic Church several years ago. After five years, things were not working out and they both felt like they didn't love each other anymore. They soon separated and got a "divorce." A year later, Martin was dating Darlene and decided to "marry" her by a judge. In the eyes of the Catholic Church, Martin is still married to Rachel, therefore he is committing adultery. This is a grave sin.

What about annulments? For a marriage to take place, a number of conditions are necessary. Some people may say that an annulment is the same as a "Church divorce;" but, this cannot be further from the truth!

An annulment is not dissolution of an existing marriage, but rather a determination, by a Catholic Diocesan Tribunal, that a marriage never existed. It is a long, difficult and painful process for the couple to go through.

The Tribunal examines each situation and the evidence presented by the parties very carefully and judges if one or both parties have given a valid consent to get married. There are numerous reasons why consent would be judged invalid.

Here are some examples: It could be that one of the parties was forced to get married, one of the parties had no intention of having children at the time of marriage or one of the parties suffers from a serious psychological condition and hides this from the other party.

2.Procreation and Education of the Children

By it's very nature, the institution of marriage and married love is ordered to the procreation and education of the offspring and it is in them that it finds its crowning glory. (CCC# 1652).

What this means is that couples who marry need to be open to life and want to welcome children into the world. *All marriage acts should be left open to the transmition of life* (*Humanae Vitae*, 11).

Again, the culture – influenced by Hollywood and other media outlets – often views or portrays children as burdens, obstacles to achieve dreams, the end of freedom. This is so far from the truth: *Children are the supreme gift of marriage and contribute greatly to the good of the parents themselves (CCC# 1652).*

It is an awesome gift to cooperate with God in the creation of a new human being. Since bringing children into the world is one of the essential properties of matrimony, any attempt to frustrate this purpose is a grave sin. Many Catholics are not aware or choose not to learn what the teachings of the Catholic Church are on contraception. In the Encyclical *Humanae Vitae,* it's made clear what the teachings of the Catholic Church are on abortion, contraception and other issues pertaining to human life. We talk about these teachings in other parts of the book. In this part we want to make you aware of the effects that contraception has in a marriage relationship.

When a husband and wife contracept, no matter which method they use, they are telling a lie with their bodies. You see, the marital act says, "I give you all of myself." If a couple uses contraception they are not saying that but are saying, "I refuse to give you all of me. You can only have part of me, but not my fertility." This may seem trivial, but it will damage the marriage. The woman will actually become an object for her husband's pleasure – just as a mistress or a prostitute. This may sound harsh but, when procreation is separated from the marital union, the dignity of the woman is continually degraded. The wife can also use her husband which, too, degrades his dignity as a person. Remember, man is the giver of love. If the love he is giving has strings attached, say by making the act infertile, the woman is actually denying his gift of love. Although folks don't realize this when they choose to contracept, this is the case. When a couple uses a barrier method for contraception, their lovemaking does not allow them to truly become one flesh because of the material that is literally between them.

The Church does not expect the married couple to have as many children as humanly possible. She asks that couples be generous in the gift of life. She asks that they prayerfully consider how many children God asks them to bring into the world. Here are some of the things She [the Church] asks them to consider for responsible parenthood:

- ✟ Physical, economic, psychological and social conditions
- ✟ Evaluate reasons for not welcoming another pregnancy
- ✟ Realize that a couple must have "serious reasons and with due respect to moral principles not to have additional children for either a certain or an indefinite period of time." (Humane Vitae)

You see, children, souls are worth so much more than material goods, vacations or an elaborate lifestyle. Therefore, when a couple decides not to have more children because they want to buy a boat, or a bigger house or car, this is not a "serious reason." What is a "serious reason?" Well, long-term unemployment, an illness or even a mother being too overwhelmed by other children. The Church asks that couples consider the question of children many times throughout their marriage. You may think that you would like to have five kids when you get married and find that when you have two you are exhausted and overwhelmed. This doesn't mean after two you decide you are done. Instead, you wait, pray and see how things progress. You will see that many times being overwhelmed passes and then you and your spouse can consider another baby once again. The opposite is true as well. You originally think you only want a small family but with prayer and discernment you change your mind and have a larger family. The key point is that God is part of that decision.

So, if a couple is not allowed to use contraception, how do they regulate births? The Church allows couples with serious reasons to avoid pregnancy to use natural family planning. This is a method that goes by the woman's reproductive cycle to determine infertile times when the couple can engage in the marital act without becoming pregnant. There are several methods available today that are accurate and easy to use. Many engaged couples learn natural family as part of their pre-wedding classes. It is easy to use but it does take self-control at times – and remember that self-control is a virtue. It is good for the marriage and it allows the spouses to revere their sexuality.

Some couples may not be blessed with children of their own. The Church teaches that *Spouses to whom God has not granted children can nevertheless have a conjugal life full of meaning, in both human and Christian terms. Their marriage can radiate fruitfulness of charity or hospitality and of sacrifice (CCC #1654).*

God may have other plans for these couples. Perhaps they are called to adoption. There are so many children who do not have parents to take care of them. Adoption is a beautiful act of self-giving! God may have other plans for a couple that doesn't have children. They may be called to do works of charity – to be very involved in parish life thereby becoming spiritual parents to many.

The Consent: I do

Some people may say *"Father so and so married us."* This is incorrect. In matrimony, the bride and the groom administer or confer the Sacrament to each other in the presence of a witness, who preferably and most commonly is a Catholic priest. The Catholic Church normally requires a marriage to take place during Holy Mass. The consent of the spouses is what "makes the marriage": You have probably been at a cousin's or a friend of the family's wedding, and have heard the bride's words, "I, Sally, take you Dan, to be my husband...." And then the groom's "I, Dan, take you Sally to be my wife..."This is the consent. The consent means *"a human act by which the partners mutually give themselves to each other"* (*CCC #1627*). If there is no consent, there is no marriage. The priest, or deacon, receives the consent of the spouses in the name of the Church and gives the bride and groom the blessing of the Church.

If God calls you to marriage, it's very critical that you and your fiancé prepare well to receive the Sacrament of Matrimony. First of all, both should make a good confession of your whole lives. You both need to understand well the purpose of marriage: the unity of the spouses and the procreation and education of the children. The Sacrament of Matrimony signifies the union of Christ and the Church. That is how you and your future spouse will strive to love each other – with a holy and supernatural love.

Mixed Marriages

A mixed marriage takes place between a Catholic and a baptized non-Catholic. A marriage with *disparity of cult* is between a Catholic and a non-baptized person. The Catholic Church does not forbid either of these marriages, but does encourage Catholics to marry other Catholics. It will make things much easier in the long run as the husband and wife have a common bond they share and that they can return to for strength and grace.

In mixed marriages and disparity of cult, *differences about faith and the very notion of marriage, but also different religious mentalities, can be sources of tension in marriage, especially as regards the education of children. The temptation to religious indifference can then arise (CCC #1634).*

Amazing Grace

Since Matrimony is a Sacrament, God grants the spouses the necessary graces to love each other faithfully, to raise their children properly, to bear each other's defects and the difficulties of married life and to sanctify each other.

Tom and Monica got married 17 years ago in Mexico City. When Monica's dad, Jaime, walked her down the aisle – where Tom was waiting for his beautiful bride – Jaime whispered something in Tom's ear. Later, Tom told Monica what her dad had told him: *"Tom, here I give you my daughter. Take her to Heaven."*

Matrimony is a vocation to sanctity – the path of both husband and wife to Heaven. It is in the little things that you will grow in holiness and help your spouse grow in holiness too: creating a cheerful home for your husband and children, greeting your husband with a smile when he comes home from work, overlooking his defects; in a few words, doing everything you do for the love of God.

Christ the Bridegroom

The nuptial covenant between God and his people Israel had prepared the way for the new and everlasting covenant in which the Son of God, by becoming incarnate and giving his life, has united to himself in a certain way all mankind saved by him, thus preparing for "the wedding-feast of the Lamb" (CCC #1612).

What great reassurance married couples have of Christ's love when He calls Himself a bridegroom! Of course this can only be truly comforting, and reveal the depth of His commitment, when we understand the context within which He spoke. We cannot look at the lack of marital commitment in today's world and fully grasp what Jesus meant when He answered the question about fasting by saying, *"Can the wedding guests mourn as long as the bridegroom is with them? The days will come when the bridegroom is taken away from them, and then they will fast."* Matthew 9:15.

What did Christ want us to understand when He used that term bridegroom? Isaiah offers a very succinct understanding of the wedded relationship Jesus would have been speaking of when He proclaimed Himself the bridegroom to us, His Church and bride. To offer, along with the words He used to portray the union between Himself and us, His bride, Christ also used the Wedding at Cana to further inculcate the idea that our relationship with Him was as indissoluble as a marriage vow.

When Christ promises to be our bridegroom, then, He is including all these understandings for He is linking the Old Covenant with the New Covenant as the fulfillment of Jeremiah 31:31-33:

> The days are coming, says the Lord, when I will make a new covenant with the house of Israel and the house of Judah. It will not be like the covenant I made with their fathers the day I took them by the hand to lead them forth from the land of Egypt; for they broke my covenant and I had to show myself their master, says the Lord. But this is the covenant which I will make with the house of Israel after those days, says the Lord. I will place my law within them, and write it upon their hearts; I will be their God, and they shall be my people.

Consider, also, the Wedding at Cana, in which Christ turned ceremonial washing water into wine. It is no coincidence that He chose this sacred event, a wedding, to bring us into His fold. Reading John 2:1-12 we cannot help but feel like treasured guests witnessing what our Lord and Savior has in store for us. He who is the best wine saved for last, the blood covenant which becomes the one sacrifice that replaces the many, makes Himself known at a wedding.

When we consider Christ making Himself known as our bridegroom, we grasp the depth of those words by understanding the original intent of marriage; the joining of a man and a woman together, forever. It is a union witnessed before God. In every way, Christ has made man aware of His enduring love but none more poignantly than in describing His great love as the love that a man and a woman share in marriage. There is a reason that this cornerstone considers Himself a bridegroom.

If you are called to the vocation of a Christian marriage, you are called to it with a spirit of service, love, endurance and commitment as witnessed by Christ our bridegroom.

Single Life

Years ago, a single woman was seen as someone who "missed the boat." People would say, "Poor thing, she couldn't find a husband." People did not realize then that single life is a vocation as much as consecrated life or marriage. Single life is not the *last choice* of one who couldn't get married.

God calls some people to remain single and still live in the world. Single people are called to refrain from sexual activity. Single women have a job or a career; some take care of their elderly parents, some help out in apostolic work, charities or parish life. Single women can make a great contribution to the growth of Christianity because of their presence and activity in all areas of life: social, economic, cultural, artistic and political.

There are women, also, who do not have a vocation to religious life or marriage but are called to be celibate for apostolic reasons. They may live with their families or wherever is convenient for professional reasons. Or they may live together with other women in a home. Their vocation is to live and work in the world while also giving their lives to God.

An example of this is Opus Dei, a Catholic institution founded by Saint Josemaría Escrivá whose mission is to spread the message that work and the circumstances of everyday life are occasions for growing closer to God, for serving others and for improving society.

Whatever you discern your vocation to be, God chose it just for you. During high school and college pray that He will show you what it is He is calling you to do with your life. Yes, my dear sister, you are being called!

...and he noticed a poor widow putting in two small coins. He said, "I tell you truly, this poor widow put in more than all the rest; for those others have all made offerings from their surplus wealth, but she, form her poverty, has offered her whole livelihood.

Luke 21:1b

Special Prayer

for

Discerning a Vocation

My Lord Jesus Christ, who did die for my salvation, I implore You, through the merits of Your passion, to give me light and strength to choose that state of life which is best for my salvation. Speak, Lord, for your servant hears.

Let me know what You wish from me, and I will do all; and let me especially know in what state You wish me to serve You; make known to me the way in which I should walk, in order to reach heaven. And you, my loving Mother Mary, obtain this grace for me through your powerful intercession.

Amen.

Scrapbooking tips

> A couple of smaller books to capture specific memories like prom or a birthday are better than one humungous scrapbook capturing, let's say, all of senior year.

> Pick a great color and work with that family and its complementary colors.

> Definitely visit a scrapbook store and some of the better sites.

> Don't be embarrassed to ask someone who has an awesome scrapbook for tips and tricks – she'll be flattered by your sincere interest in her work!

Capture your precious memories, today, in a fun way!

Virtues to
Live By

Human virtues are good habits that incline you to do what is right. You acquire virtues by a continuous exercise of good actions: you train yourself. Some examples of human virtues are: order, generosity, responsibility, chastity, modesty and simplicity.

The Virtue of Simplicity

Natalie is jealous because her best friend, Cindy, just got eyeglasses and is getting plenty of compliments on them. She lies to her parents about not being able to see right and needing eyeglasses herself. Of course, what she wants is attention, and not being left behind in popularity.

Cynthia has always wanted to fit in with the popular kids in her high school. Even though she has always dressed plain and simple, she decides to go for the sophisticated look so that she can be accepted.

Brianna has trouble in math class. She decides to befriend Laura, who is all brains, so that she gets an A in math this semester. After school is over, Brianna dumps Laura because she doesn't *need* her anymore.

Jessica literally *makes mountains out of molehills.* If one day you accidentally forget to say "hi" to her in school, she automatically assumes you are upset with her. If you didn't answer her call, she thinks you are hiding from her. She is on an emotional roller-coaster.

Haley is part of a Bible youth group and loves it. When she gets together with her school friends, however, she denies having anything to do with Bible groups. She tosses her Christian convictions aside because she is afraid her school friends are going to make fun of her.

Do you identify yourself with any of these girls? These girls are examples of a person who lacks the virtue of simplicity.

The lack of simplicity expresses itself through behavior, dress and/or speech:

Behavior:

Pretending to be who you are not; pretending to have material things or talents to attract attention or to fit in; giving people the "cold shoulder;" not being able to let go of past offenses; having "multiple personalities" depending on what group of people you are with;

Dress:

Wearing fashions that do not reflect your dignity as a daughter of God; wearing certain clothes to give the impression you are better off than others; not willing to dress up for the occasion (for example, attending a wedding in your blue jeans);

Speech:

Taking over a conversation and making it all about you; always having a better story than anyone else; pretending you have all the answers – that you know it all; talking bad about your friend behind her back; twisting the truth to get what you want;

Simplicity, on the other hand, is a great virtue that encompasses things such as:

- ✝ Letting yourself be known as you really are
- ✝ Having the courage to stand up for what is right
- ✝ Being genuine, authentic and free from pretense or hypocrisy.
- ✝ Assuming the best about people
- ✝ Saying what you really mean
- ✝ Being happy for your friends' accomplishments
- ✝ Being happy to be YOU – not having a need to copy others

For you to acquire this virtue, you need to be yourself. Simplicity starts in one's heart; what's in your heart will be reflected in your behavior, dress and speech.

So the question becomes: What *is* in your heart? Is it love, joy and a desire to please God? Or is it selfishness, sadness and a desire to please yourself? Have you ever met someone who radiates joy, peace, is confident of herself and enjoys life? People like that are pleasures to be with! People like that live the virtue of simplicity.

You'll need to focus on "cleaning up" your heart first. When doing Spring-cleaning, people get rid of tons of junk. Well, the same way here, you need to get rid of:

✟ Self pity trips: *poor me, nobody appreciates me...*

✟ Jumping to conclusions about other people's words or behaviors

✟ Jealousy towards a friend's accomplishment or material possessions

✟ Desire to stand out – to be noticed

✟ Seeing the glass as "half empty"

✟ Only doing things if there is something in it for you

Once that's done, focus on your good qualities and ask Jesus how you can be more "like Him." Every created person has special gifts, and so do you. Are you naturally kind? Or organized? Or perhaps you love to help people? Discern through prayer what your qualities are and what qualities God would like you to acquire.

Many teens lack the virtue of simplicity because they want to fit in with their peers, they want to be accepted, and therefore they put on a "mask" to meet their peers' expectations. When you realize your dignity as a daughter of God, you won't care about what other's think, you won't be dying to fit in certain groups. You will have self confidence and you will be happy to be yourself. And what's even better is that others will know you and love you as you truly are – a daughter of the King with unique gifts and talents!

Perseverance as a virtue...

Perseverance is achieving the goal you have set for yourself in spite of difficulties such as tiredness, boredom, impatience or discouragement. It's the opposite of "throwing in the towel." Laziness is the opposite of perseverance. It's giving up when you get tired. It's changing your mind when you see the obstacles in your way. Perseverance is sticking to your commitments such as picking up your bedroom or volunteering at your parish picnic despite the hardships you may encounter such as low pay, being hot or bored. Sometimes you may need to give up other more interesting activities in order to stick to your commitment.

For instance, you promised your Grandma you would rake the leaves in her yard, but your friend Mindy asks you to go to a movie with her. You would honor your promise to Grandma if you chose to persevere. Having a goal in mind is the key to perseverance. Once you have a goal, you make a plan to achieve it, and take into account the likelihood of obstacles you may encounter. That way when they happen, you will be prepared to overcome them. You won't be tempted to quit or feel discouraged. What's the reason of having a goal in the first place? Well, it should be to give glory to God in all you do and that should be reason enough to help you persevere.

Kindness as a virtue...

Kindness is the act of being gracious and charitable towards other people. It is characterized by goodness, affection, gentleness, consideration and the disposition to help others. The world needs kindness! By being kind, you have the power to make the world a happier place in which to live.

Kindness is inspired in your love for God as Jesus tells us in Matthew 22: "You shall love the Lord your God with all your heart, with all your soul, with all your strength and with all your mind." When you love God with all your being, that love outpours into love for others; bitterness, sarcasm and meanness disappear. As Jesus has said, "Love your neighbor as yourself." When you are kind, you put others in the place of yourself and you treat them in the way you would like to be treated. In order to be kind, you need to be sure that your actions, words and thoughts are kind.

Purity as a virtue...

The ultimate goal of every person is to get to Heaven. How do you get there? Purity of the heart is the way. How do you know this? Jesus says, "Blessed are the pure of heart for they shall see God." A pure heart includes your thoughts, intentions, curiosity, and judgment of others. To have a clean heart you must always try to get rid of bad thoughts and keep your judgments and intentions good. When you are curious about everyone's business, it is a sign that your heart needs some clean up. Knowing everyone else's business can fuel your imagination and take it away from pure thoughts.

Purity means filling your own mind with thoughts of Jesus. Instead of being curious about other people's personal business, spend time contemplating what it means being a daughter of the King. These are the kinds of thoughts that lead to a pure heart for Christ.

Human virtues are firm attitudes, stable dispositions, habitual perfections of intellect and will that govern our actions, order our passions and guide our conduct according to reason and faith. They make possible ease, self-mastery and joy in leading a morally good life. The virtuous man is he who freely practices the good (CCC #1804).

There are many wonderful Catholic women – throughout time – who display virtues through their everyday lives.

Think about the times when your mom displays kindness or patience even though she may be at her wit's end! Or how about your grandmother or aunt who always make sure to pray the rosary and do volunteer work at the local nursing home or pregnancy center. You, too, can grow into a virtuous woman if you just make the commitment today.

Our faith is filled with virtuous women who lived many years ago or are living today. These are the sorts of role models you want to emulate.

Check them out:

- ✟ St. Helena is the mother of Constantine, the emperor who legalized Christianity in the Roman Empire. She worked to convert him and he was baptized before his death. She is believed to have found the true cross of Jesus.
- ✟ St. Hunna married a nobleman of France, she was generous and helpful to the poor and underprivileged. She was known as the "Holy Washerwoman" for doing menial tasks despite her social status.
- ✟ St. Olga was a peasant who married Igor, Grand Duke of Russia. After her baptism she desired to convert her son and her country. Although she didn't accomplish this, her grandson Vladimir did because of her influence on him before her death.

Brenda Sharman

Brenda Sharman and her husband Steve live in Atlanta, Georgia with their three sons. Brenda grew up in a non-Christian household and when she was in high school, she began modeling and acting, which became her profession that she still is active in today. She has been in many magazines and commercials over the years. In 1990, Brenda entered her first beauty contest and won Miss Georgia USA.

After the birth of her first son, Brenda began soul searching. This search led her to the Catholic Church and in 1999 she became a Catholic and her life changed forever! For one thing, she no longer felt comfortable modeling underwear or lingerie and began to refuse these types of modeling jobs and commercials.

Today, Brenda is using her expertise as a model and her experience in the world of fashion to help educate and form teen aged girls on the dignity of the person. She began an apostolate called Pure Fashion. Pure Fashion is no ordinary style show. It is a 6-8 month training session for young women which covers topics such as public speaking, manners, hair, makeup, modesty and personal presentation. Throughout the program, purity of heart, mind and body are emphasized. At the end of the training the girls are models in a city wide fashion show. Cities such as Chicago, Seattle, and Atlanta were some of the first places to host Pure Fashion programs.

If you are interested in getting involved in Pure Fashion you can check and see if your city has a program by going to www.purefashion.com. If it doesn't, maybe your mom and her friends can start it in your town!

Brenda is a beautiful example of the feminine genius. She is using her gifts to further the Kingdom of God.

Vicki Thorn

Vicki Thorn started Project Rachel in Milwaukee, Wisconsin in 1984. She was one of the first ever to help women with post-abortion trauma. In the 1980's she was a young mother with a psychology degree who wanted to help friends she knew who were suffering after having an abortion. Today she has six children, is a trauma counselor, and a facilitator in bereavement loss and prenatal loss.

Project Rachel is a diocesan-based ministry that includes clergy with special training, spiritual directors, and therapists who help women and men who have been involved in abortion in any way. She wasn't expecting Project Rachel to grow outside her diocese, especially because the counseling profession denied that women and others were negatively affected by an abortion. Today she travels nationally and internationally speaking on post-abortion trauma.

Think about it, we all make mistakes but think of a mistake that would change your life. Abortion is such a mistake. Not only does the baby suffer, but also anyone who is involved: the father, grandparents, bothers, sisters and friends. Women and men who are post-abortive have terrible guilt. Project Rachel helps them to heal and to forgive themselves.

The first thing Project Rachel does is put the person in touch with a priest who has had special training. There is such a burden lifted when the person can go to confession and know they are forgiven. So many women who have been helped by Project Rachel go on to understand the Church's teaching on abortion and even other teachings they rejected. Think of the impact this program has had on people! Vicki Thorn has trained between 4,000-5,000 clergy to aid in Project Rachel. Wow, one person can make a difference!

And then there was a time long, long ago...

Many hundreds of years ago there was a woman named Ruth. She was married to one of the sons of Naomi. Naomi was a Jewish woman who loved God so much that she made Ruth see how good it was to love God. Sadly, Naomi's sons died and so did  Naomi's husband. This meant that Naomi only had two daughters-in-law left in her family. At that time Naomi was living in a land that was not her home. She was living in a place called Moab and Ruth was from Moab. Ruth was called a "Moabite."

What is so amazing about Ruth's story was that she was considered an "outsider." Because she didn't, at first, believe in the one true God, people didn't think of her as belonging to their crowd or culture. But remember that Naomi was a great witness to Ruth. This means that Naomi lived her life in such a way as people could look at her and sort of see a "walking bible."

Anyhow, once Naomi's sons died, Naomi encouraged her daughters-in-law to stay in their homeland of Moab but that she, herself, was going to return to her own homeland, Bethlehem. Naomi and her family had left Bethlehem because of a famine but now word was out that there was food in the land so she was going to go home.

Travelling back then was not like it is today. There were no planes to board nor any buses or cars. Travel took weeks and months and was very difficult. So, when Naomi announced that she would go back to Bethlehem, it was quite surprising for Ruth to insist on going with her. Not only was it going to be a long and rough trip but Ruth really wouldn't be welcomed in Bethlehem because she was an outsider. But Ruth couldn't be deterred. That means she couldn't be held back from doing what she wanted to do which was stay with her mother-in-law, Naomi. This is what Ruth said to Naomi...

> *Do not ask me to abandon or forsake you! For wherever you go I will go, where you lodge I will lodge, your people shall be my people, and your God my God. Wherever you die I will die and there be buried. May the Lord do so and so to me, and more besides, if aught but death separates me from you!*

Wow, those are pretty powerful words, aren't they? Can you imagine how Naomi must have witnessed to Ruth to make Ruth so in love with Naomi's God, your God? But the story gets even better.

Once Ruth and Naomi were back in Bethlehem, Ruth met a man named Boaz. He was a distant relative of Naomi's and looked upon Ruth with love. He wanted to marry her and when he made his intentions known all his friends and family gave him their blessings. This is what they said...

> *May the Lord make this wife come into your house like Rachel and Leah, who between them built up the house of Israel. May you do well and win fame in Bethlehem.*

Ruth and Boaz's story is one of real true love and also the story of Jesus. Why? Because Ruth and Boaz had a son they named Obed. Obed then grew up and had a son named Jesse. Jesse is the father of David who became king and is the family tree in which Jesus Christ is born!

Etiquette

Practicing good etiquette is a wonderful way to practice charity and kindness. For instance, it is good etiquette to say "Please" and "Thank-you" while those are also good and kind things to say to others.

Here are a few etiquette lessons that every daughter of the King should know and practice.

Words, words, words.

They make up your daily communication with others. You use them to greet people, to compliment others, to express your feelings and opinions and even to complain! Words are very important. They can define the outcome of a situation. It is important for you to know that the words you use with your friends may not be the right words to use while talking to some adults.

Nice to Meet You!

Meeting new people is great! The way you greet them says a lot about your person. If you are introduced to someone and you are

looking down to the ground while shaking their hand means that you don't really care to meet them.

So, what's the proper way to greet somebody new?

- ✝ It is important to make eye contact. It shows people that you are honest and that you are interested in them.
- ✝ Listen very carefully for the person's name and repeat it as you are being introduced, "Nice to meet you, Mrs. Welsch." Repeating the person's name will help you remember it later.
- ✝ Shake hands with a firm grip when you are saying hello to an adult.

What about introductions? Here are some situations where you will need to play the role of "Introducer:"

✝ You just arrived at the movie theater with your friend Heather, and there you bump into Sheila, your neighbor. What do you do? Well, you need to introduce them to each other! "Heather, this is my neighbor, Sheila." "Sheila, this is my friend Heather." It's that easy!

✝ Your friend Amanda comes to your house for the first time. It is important that you introduce her to your parents right away.

Attempt Words

Hmm...Nah...Huh? We call these "attempt" words because they are a lame attempt at conversing! They are words that have nothing to do with a conversation and are best avoided.

Imagine this conversation between friends:

> -Wanna c'me?
> -Hmm....Nah!
> -Huh?
> -Ok, Yeah!

Who really knows what they were saying! There are situations where the use of "attempt" words is rude, such as talking to adults like your teachers, a boss, or a parish priest.

Swear Words and Put Down Words

These words are designed to insult and offend people. But chances are you already knew that! They make conversations nasty. Remember that as a daughter of the King you want to use words that reflect your dignity, your royalty. You want to use words that uplift others, not put them down. Think about the Blessed Mother and imagine how she talked to the people around her. She must have used kind words in her conversations; she complimented people and was kind. That's who you need to imitate!

Virtuous speaking means choosing words carefully and with wisdom. Here are a few pointers:

- ✠ If you can't say something nice, don't say anything at all.
- ✠ Vulgar language is NOT an option.
- ✠ Swearing is a NO-NO.
- ✠ Dirty jokes are to be avoided. If someone tells one around you, either walk away or say something like, "Not good...," "That's disgusting!" or "Keep it to yourself next time."
- ✠ Conversation about personal bodily functions is tacky, so skip it.
- ✠ Talking about personal "girl" stuff should be done privately.

As a rule of thumb, if you couldn't say it in front of our Blessed Mother, don't say it. Remember, she's in Heaven and would hear you anyway! One day we all will have to give an accounting of ourselves, before God, of every word that has been said. That should cause some serious hesitation before speaking!

A Plan
for
Life

You, the Human Person

The human person, created in the image of God, is a being at once corporal and spiritual (CCC #362).

Yes, you are a human person, the unity of body and soul. And you were from your conception! That means that every embryo is a human person and no matter how much other people try to change or distort this Truth, the Church teaches that God creates the soul *immediately at the moment of conception*, and that the soul *is immortal: it does not perish when it separates from the body at the time of death, and it will be reunited with the body at the final Resurrection* (CCC #366).

This is awesome to know but also bears great responsibility in regards to your own behavior and keeping chaste and also in knowing that you can help protect unborn babies by sharing this Truth with others.

As a daughter of God, you are called to take care of your body and soul. The needs of your body are easy to figure out: you get hungry, therefore you need food; you get tired and sleepy, therefore you need to rest; you get thirsty, therefore you need a drink. This is because your body is physical. This means that you get to know your body's needs through your senses.  Maybe your stomach growls when you are hungry or you feel lightheaded when you are too hot and tired.

Your soul is a bit trickier to figure out, because it's the part of you that animates your body, and since it's spiritual, it's not tangible. But you are called to take care of it as much as you do your body. In the same way that you spend time every day nourishing your body through eating, resting, and exercising; you need to spend time every day nourishing your soul. You don't just eat a meal on Sunday, right? You eat every day, and several times every day. Well, it's the same way with your soul; you get the idea.

As you nourish your soul you fulfill the purpose for which you were created: to know, love and serve God. Why is this? It's because the human soul *refers to the innermost aspect of man, that which is of greatest value in him, that by which he is most especially in God's image* (CCC #363). In a few words, your soul is the part of you that is "like" God, who is all spirit. So, let's take a good look at how much time you are spending every day to nourish your soul. Perhaps you say a few prayers before you go to bed? That's good, but it's not enough.

Here is a daily plan that will help you nourish your soul. This plan is made up of several practices of piety that have been a very important part in the Tradition of the Church. None of them are new! The saints all lived or at least tried to live these practices of piety because they realized how necessary they are for one's soul to grow in union with God.

One more thing: it is important that you try to spread these practices of piety throughout your day. Think of them as on-going "pit stops" to connect with God. If you do so, you will live in the presence of God in between these practices as well.

Morning Offering

Have you ever thought of every new day as a gift from God? It's like starting a new page in your notebook. And what a better way than to start your day by offering to God everything you will do, think and say? More than just a "thing to do," the morning offering is an attitude of service and dedication to God that begins at the very moment you wake up. It sets the tone for your day. So, how do you do this? Since offering your day to God is very personal, each person will do it in his or her own way. However, it's recommended that you kneel down, right next to your bed if you'd like to, and spend a few minutes telling Our Lord that you want to please Him in everything you do, think and say. Talk to Him from your heart: *"Lord, I offer you the hours I'll spend at school; please help me on my algebra test; also, I offer to you my time at work after school; help me be cheerful with my co-worker, sometimes it's very hard..."* Ask the Blessed Mother to be with you through the day and keep you company and also ask your Guardian Angel to help and protect you. There are also beautiful prayers that were written to help people offer their day to God; here is one:

O Jesus,
through the Immaculate Heart of Mary,
I offer You my prayers, works,
joys and sufferings
of this day for all the intentions
of Your Sacred Heart,
in union with the Holy Sacrifice of the Mass
throughout the world,
in reparation for my sins,
for the intentions of all my relatives and
friends,
and in particular
for the intentions of the Holy Father.
Amen.

Whichever way you choose to offer your day to God, keep in mind throughout the day that everything you are doing is your gift for God; therefore you want to do it cheerfully and to the best of your ability. You can't – you wouldn't – offer your best friend something done sloppily! The same is with God! He doesn't deserve less than your very best.

Mental Prayer

Prayer consists of speaking to God as you would speak to your closest friend. You can pray together with a group of people, or you can pray by yourself. Mental prayer refers to your personal prayer, a heart-to-heart talk with God. You and God alone. You tell him what worries you, what is making you happy; you ask for His help, you beg His forgiveness. You express gratitude for the ways in which He cares about all the little details of your life. By speaking to God, you get to know Him and get to know His will. But prayer is a conversation. Like when you are talking to a friend, part of the time you talk and part of the time you listen; who likes to hang out with someone who is talking non-stop and hardly let's you get a word in? Well, it's the same way in prayer. You open your heart to listen to whatever God is trying to tell you. This is no easy task because sometimes you will be distracted by whatever is going on around you (noises, images and movement) or inside you (thoughts, memories and your imagination).

It takes time to grow deeper in your mental prayer, but the only way to get there is by making the time to pray every day. If you are consistent, you will start looking forward to this precious, daily time with Jesus and you will notice that the days that you neglect your prayer don't go as well as the days you give priority to your mental prayer.

Here are a few practical tips for doing mental prayer:

✟ First of all, plan ahead. Find out what time of the day works best for you. If you can do it in the morning, before you start school or work that's great. Sometimes when you leave things for the end of the day, half of the time you end up not doing them! Decide ahead of time how much time you will spend in your mental prayer every day. Ten minutes is a good goal for starters.

✝ Find a place where you can pray without distractions: away from the TV, computer, ipod, phone etc. If it's possible, pray in front of the Blessed Sacrament, it's very powerful!

✝ Start off by placing yourself in the presence of God. Realize that you are His daughter and that He is there to hear you and to love you.

✝ Share with God what's going on in your life. What's happening at school? At home? With your friends? What are your struggles? How are you reacting to disappointments? How can you use all the events in your life to grow closer to Him?

✝ Sometimes it's helpful to read parts of the New Testament to help you have a conversation with God. You can meditate on the life of Our Lord: take, for instance, the beatitudes that Jesus taught during the Sermon on the Mount. You could read one at a time and apply them to your life. The writings of the saints and other spiritual reading books are also great resources for mental prayer. Read a paragraph or so, and talk to Our Lord about it, asking Him to help you apply it to your life.

✝ Sometimes you may want to select a topic for your conversation with God.: take, for instance, a virtue you need to work on, a defect you are trying to overcome, a friend you are trying to bring closer to Him. Talk to God about it from the bottom of your heart and ask Him to inspire you to find ways to do His will in this particular topic.

✝ Once 10 minutes has passed, be sure to end your prayer with some resolutions (the Holy Spirit will guide you on this if you ask).

The following are opening and closing prayers by Saint Josemaria, for placing yourself in the presence of God and for finishing your mental prayer:

My Lord and my God, I firmly believe that you are here, that you see me, that you hear me; I adore you with profound reverence; I ask you pardon for my sins, and the grace to make this time of prayer fruitful. My Immaculate Mother, Saint Joseph my father and lord, my Guardian Angel, intercede for me.

I give you thanks Almighty God for the good resolutions, affections and inspirations that you have communicated to me in this time of prayer. I ask you to help me put them into effect. My immaculate Mother, Saint Joseph my father and lord, my Guardian Angel, intercede for me.

Reading the New Testament

How do you fall in love with a stranger? You simply don't! You gotta get to know the person before you fall in love with Him. If you want to fall in love with Jesus, you gotta get to know Him, right? The best way to know Jesus is by reading the New Testament. You are probably familiar with most of the Gospel readings, because you hear them at Sunday Mass. Still, have you ever read the New Testament cover to cover? It's fascinating!

Try to set a time every day, to read a little bit of the New Testament. It can be a chapter, which usually takes 2-3 minutes to read. The important thing is that you are consistent in doing it every day. Again, find the time of the day that is going to work out best: perhaps as soon as you get home from school or in the evening first thing after supper – whatever works for you. Reading the teachings and life of Jesus will be a great help to identify yourself with His will. Also, it'll give you material for your time of mental prayer and contemplation.

Spiritual Reading

If you want to be a great cook, I bet you'd be looking up for recipes of all kinds and new cookbooks; or if you are interested in home decorating, you'll be going through tons of magazines to get ideas, right? If you are striving to grow in holiness, you need to nourish your soul by reading books that inspire you and help you learn more about God and the Catholic Faith.

There is a saying that says: "If you want to be a saint, you need to read the stuff of saints." How true this is! If you devote 10 minutes a day to do spiritual reading, by the end of the year you will have taken a great step!

A spiritual reading book is not your Parish bulletin or your diocesan newspaper. A spiritual reading book is a book that will inspire you to desire holiness, it's a book that will help you form your conscience and enrich you in your knowledge of the faith. It is a book that enforces your values as a daughter of the King.

Here are some examples of spiritual, inspirational reading:

- ✞ *The Catechism of the Catholic Church* – a must!
- ✞ *Behold Your Mother,* Heidi Hess Saxton, Bezalel Books, 2008.
- ✞ *Blessed Gianna Beretta Molla: A Woman's Life, 1992-1962,* Giuliana Pelucchi, Pauline Books and Media, 2002.
- ✞ *Daily Direction for Teenz,* Catherine Wasson Brown, Bezalel Books, 2008.
- ✞ *Debt-Proof Living* (Rev. ed.), Mary Hunt, DPL Press, Inc., 2005.
- ✞ *The Faith Explained,* Leo Trese, Scepter Publishers, 2000.
- ✞ *Frequent Confession: Its Place in the Spiritual Life,* Benedict Baur, Scepter Publishers, 1999.
- ✞ *Friends of God,* Saint Josemaria Escriva, Sceptor Publishers.
- ✞ *The Hidden Power of Kindness: A Practical Handbook for Souls Who Dare to Transform the World, One Deed at a Time,* Lawrence Lovasik, Sophia Institute Press, 1999.
- ✞ *The Imitation of Christ,* Thomas à. Kempis, MobileReference, 2008.
- ✞ *Jesus as Friend,* Salvador Canals, Scepter Publishers.
- ✞ *Life of Christ* (2nd ed.), Fulton J. Sheen, Image, 1977.
- ✞ *Newsflash: My Surprising Journey from Secular Anchor to Media Evangelist,* Teresa Tomeo, Bezalel Books, 2008 – she's a co-author of this book!

✤ *Story of a Soul: The Autobiography of St. Therese of Lisieux* (3rd ed.), I C S Publications, 1996.

✤ *The Story of Peace*, Miriam Ezeh, Bezalel Books, 2007 – an excellent, inspirational fiction that has love and war and romance.

✤ *Walk New: A New Way of the Cross for Teens*, Kathryn, Mulderink, Bezalel Books, 2008.

Another way you can do spiritual reading is by listening to CD's while you are driving. Many of these great books are available in a CD format and both you and your mom or dad are sure to enjoy them during some of your car rides doing errands, etc.

The Angelus

The word "Angelus" means angel in Latin, and it's a beautiful devotion in memory of the Incarnation. This devotion was traditionally recited in Catholic Churches, convents and monasteries three times every day: 6:00 am, noon, and 6:00 pm. It was usually accompanied by the ringing of the bells. The Angelus is still recited by many Catholics around the world at noon.

The Angelus consists in reciting three Biblical verses and their responses describing the mystery of the Incarnation.

V. The angel of the Lord announced unto Mary.
R. And she conceived by the Holy Spirit.

Hail Mary...

V. Behold the handmaid of the Lord.
R. Be it unto me according to your Word.

Hail Mary...

V. And the Word was made flesh.
R. And dwelt among us.

Hail Mary...

V. Pray for us, O Holy Mother of God.
R. That we may be made worthy of the promises of Christ.

Let us pray: We beseech you, O Lord, pour your grace into our hearts, that as we have known the incarnation of your Son Jesus Christ by the message of an angel, so by his cross and passion we may be brought to the glory of his resurrection; through the same Christ our Lord. Amen.

Get in the habit of praying the Angelus every day. It's an easy practice of piety that can be said practically anywhere and it only takes a few minutes, but how much can you gain from it!

The Holy Rosary

Our Lady's favorite devotion is the Rosary, which means "crown of roses." John Paul II wrote in his 2002 Apostolic Letter on the Most Holy Rosary that to recite the Holy Rosary is nothing other than to contemplate with Mary the face of Christ. Some people claim that they don't pray the rosary because to do so, would be to worship Mary, the Blessed Mother. They couldn't be farther from the truth! The center of the Rosary is Christ, that's why the rosary is called a "Christocentric prayer."

In the rosary, vocal prayer (reciting the Our Father, Hail Mary, Glory Be, etc.) is combined with contemplative prayer (meditation of the mysteries in the life of Jesus). John Paul II called the Rosary a compendium of the Gospel. The mysteries you contemplate while praying the rosary take you from the annunciation of the Angel Gabriel to Mary (the beginning of the Gospels) through his birth, baptism, public life, passion, death and resurrection.

This is why the late Pope called it a compendium of the Gospel!

The rosary is divided into four mysteries, each one referring to a particular time in Jesus' life. These are the Joyful, Luminous, Sorrowful and Glorious mysteries. Each mystery has five decades, and for each decade one Our Father, 10 Hail Mary's and the Glory Be are said.

Rosary Details

Although having rosary beads in your hands is not a requirement to say this beautiful prayer to Our Lady, it's always of great help to keep track of the number of Hail Mary's and the mysteries. In this way your mind is free to meditate on the mysteries instead of counting. You can also use your fingers and/or knots on a string to count.

- ✝ Make the sign of the cross on the Crucifix and then say the Apostles Creed
- ✝ Pray an Our Father on the first large bead
- ✝ Pray a Hail Mary on each of the three small beads with the following intentions (the theological virtues):
    1. For the increase of faith
    2. For the increase of hope
    3. For the increase of charity
- ✝ Pray a Glory Be to the Father
- ✝ Announce the mystery
- ✝ Pray an Our Father on the large bead
- ✝ Pray a Hail Mary on each of the adjacent ten small beads
- ✝ Pray a Glory Be to the Father followed by the Fatima Prayer (it follows)
- ✝ Again pray an Our Father on the next large bead, followed by ten Hail Marys on the small beads, the Glory Be to the Father and Fatima Prayer for each of the following decades;
- ✝ In conclusion, "Hail Holy Queen" and a sign of the cross.

Fatima prayer:
Oh my Jesus, forgive us our sins, save us from the fires of hell; lead all the souls to Heaven, especially those who are in most need of Your mercy.

Each mystery is said on a certain day of the week, that way each week you'll be meditating on Jesus' whole life:

- ♱ Sunday – Glorious
- ♱ Monday – Joyful
- ♱ Tuesday – Sorrowful
- ♱ Wednesday – Glorious
- ♱ Thursday – Luminous
- ♱ Friday – Sorrowful
- ♱ Saturday – Joyful

The Rosary is a very powerful prayer; the Blessed Mother has made specific promises to Christians who pray the Rosary. Among these promises are: special graces, protection from misfortune, a higher degree of glory in Heaven, assistance at the time of death and deliverance from Purgatory.

If you are not saying the Rosary every day, begin by saying one or two decades a day. It doesn't take long! You can pray while going for a walk, waiting for an appointment or driving in a car. This is one of the beauties of the Rosary: it can be prayed almost everywhere! Gradually increase the number of decades until you say a complete set of five decades

Holy Mass

You know already that attending Mass is one of the most important things for a Catholic. It's actually one of the Commandments to attend Mass on Sundays and Holy Days of Obligation. The Mass is the Sacrifice of the New Covenant, in which Christ, through the ministry of the priest, offers Himself to God in an unbloody manner under the appearance of bread and wine. This is why the

Mass has infinite value; therefore, you need to attend Mass with reverence, attention and devotion.

The purposes of the Mass are: to adore God as our Creator, to thank God for His many blessings, to ask God for our needs and to ask God for forgiveness for our sins. The fruits of attending are the following: grace to repent of mortal sin, forgiveness of venial sin and remission of the temporal punishment due to sin. These fruits are granted to those who hear Mass devoutly. This means that you pay attention to the readings and prayers, participate by praying, watch your posture when sitting, standing and kneeling, and have an overall interior attitude of union with God. Now ask yourself: "Do I attend Mass devoutly, or do I just "show up" and think that fulfills my obligation?"

At Mass you can receive the Eucharist if you are in the state of grace – that means with no mortal sin on your soul. The Eucharist is the Body and Blood of Our Lord Jesus Christ. This is the most awesome gift that we Catholics have!

Tyler, who was a fundamentalist, asked his Catholic friend, Patrick, the following question: *"If you Catholics truly believe that Jesus is present with His Body, Blood, Soul and Divinity in the Eucharist, why don't you guys do everything possible to attend Mass every day in order to receive Him?"*

Tyler has a good point! What about you? You can't be content with doing the bare minimum!

Daily Examination of Conscience

If you have had a job working at a store or fast food place, you probably know that at the end of the day it's important to make an inventory of items and balance the drawer. If this is not done, its' very hard to get an idea of how well the business is doing, and also to get an idea of what's in stock. Is there a need to order more hamburger patties, or are there enough in the freezer? Are the profits bigger than the expenses? Keeping track of these things is critical to the success of any business.

Well, the state of your soul is probably the most important "business" you will ever have to manage. The daily examination of conscience is like "balancing the books" or "checking inventory" in your soul. It needs to be done every day in order to make progress in your road to holiness. But, how do you do that? There are different ways of examining your conscience. The important thing is that you place yourself in the presence of God and take a look at your day.

You can ask yourself the following questions:

✝ What did I do today that was pleasing to you, Jesus? Perhaps you controlled your temper when your brother pestered you, or you offered your mom help making supper without being asked. Be sure to thank Jesus for the graces He sent your way in order for you to do these good deeds.

✝ What did I do today that was not pleasing to you, Jesus? It could be that you spent too much time on the computer, or talked bad behind your friend's back. Once you recall the things that did not please Jesus, make sure to say sorry in your own words or by saying –and meaning- the act of contrition.

✝ What would you like me to do better tomorrow? You try to come up with a resolution for the next day, such as, "Tomorrow I'm going to cut down the time I spend on the computer and instead I'll give attention to my younger sister."

Ask the Holy Spirit to help you be humble and sincere. Sometimes it's very helpful to have some sort of journal or notebook, where you can write down the results of your daily exam. In this way you'll be able to see, after a couple of weeks, which areas you are weaker in and which areas need improvement. Writing things down is also a great aid to help you prepare for confession, because you won't have to try to remember so far back.

Make sure to use the accompanying *All Things Girl: Truth for Teens Journal* to chart your prayer life.

Get to Know Our Lady

Mary is the most perfect creature that came from God's hands because Mary was exempt from original sin; she was full of grace from her conception. She is the Immaculate Conception.

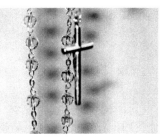

From a very young age, Mary entrusted her whole life to do God's will. At the Annunciation, the Angel Gabriel revealed to her the purpose for which she was created: to give birth and to take care of Jesus, the Second Person of the Holy Trinity. Wow! Imagine that! From then on, she lived every moment of her life to fulfill that purpose. She corresponded to all the graces she received from God. Mary was very young when she gave birth to Jesus, perhaps she was your age, or a little younger.

It's easy to get close to Mary because she lived a very ordinary life. She was a homemaker, therefore she had to wash clothes, prepare meals and clean the house for Joseph and Jesus, as millions of homemakers do in our day. She did all the same mundane chores but without modern conveniences. For instance, she didn't have a microwave to heat up Joseph's coffee or a washing machine to do the laundry. There was no running water in the house, no air conditioning or furnace, so she suffered from the heat and was chilled by the cold. To travel she rode a donkey or walked.

Our Lady had the fullness of virtue. She stands out for her humility. She never made a big fuss about being the Mother of God in order to impress people or to get what she wanted; she did not demand to be treated in a special manner, nor to have special privileges. Take, for instance, the journey with Joseph to Bethlehem. Her time came to deliver baby Jesus, and they were forced to find a place to stay. Mary could have complained, "Hey, how come I have to go through this? I'm carrying Jesus, the Messiah in my womb; I should be entitled to royal treatment." But she didn't complain; she humbly accepted God's will. She was cheerful and patient.

The best way to get to know Our Lady and deepen your devotion to her is to learn more about her. The Gospels, found in the New Testament, narrate various scenes in the life of Our Lady, from which you can learn about her. You see her courage in saying "yes" to God's call to receive Jesus in her womb; or her silent obedience to God's will when she and Joseph had to flee Egypt; or her love for her cousin Elizabeth, that made her travel all the way to help her; her concern at the Wedding feast at Cana, when they were running out of wine and it was going to be very embarrassing for the bride and groom; her strength in being at the foot of the Cross.

Read these passages from the Gospels and ponder them in your heart. You actually do this when you pray the Rosary. Ask Our Lady to teach you how to be humble, patient, and pure – for she is the ideal role model. When you are faced with a difficult situation, ask her: "How would you have handled this?" See, if you want to get closer to a certain person, you need to spend time getting to know each other. It's the same way with our Lady; you need to spend time with her.

It was at the foot of the Cross that Jesus gave us Mary to be our Mother. *Standing by the cross of Jesus were his mother and his mother's sister, Mary the wife of Clopas, and Mary of Magdala. When Jesus saw his mother and the disciple there whom he loved, he said to his mother, "Woman, behold, your son." Then he said to the disciple, "Behold, your mother." And from that hour the disciple took her into his home.* (John 19:25-27). The Church has always seen John as representing all Christians, you included. Jesus, after giving himself to us, wished to give us her whom He loved the most: Our Blessed Mother. And, in the same way that she took care of Jesus, she will take care of you if you entrust yourself to her loving protection.

Your life, like Mary's, is a journey of faith, in which you are called to fulfill freely the mission for which you were created. Mary imitated Jesus in a way that no other creature has. The best way to imitate Jesus is to imitate Our Lady. JPII is said to have had a very special relationship with Mary. He loved her and counted on her constant intercession. Walk your journey with Mary and you'll have the assurance you are on the right track!

Behold Your Mother,
by Heidi Hess Saxton,
is a great book to help you meditate
upon the life of Mary.
Her many titles are contemplated and each has a
corresponding Scripture verse.

Lovely Lady Dressed in Blue
By Mary Dixon Thayer

Lovely Lady dressed in blue
Teach me how to pray!
God was just your little boy,
Tell me what to say!

Did you lift Him up, sometimes,
Gently on your knee?
Did you sing to Him the way
Mother does to me?

Did you hold His hand at night?
Did you ever try
Telling stories of the world?
O! And did He cry?

Do you really think He cares
If I tell Him things
Little things that happen? And
Do the Angels' wings
Make a noise? And can He hear
Me if I speak low?
Does He understand me now?
Tell me, for you know.

Lovely Lady dressed in blue
Teach me how to pray!
God was just your little boy,
And you know the way.

A word about Confession

How is it that nowadays everybody goes to Communion during Mass, while very, very few people go to Confession? There was a time, not too long ago, where people would never dream of receiving Communion without having confessed their sins and received absolution first. So, is it that people don't sin anymore? Or, is it that people *think* they don't sin anymore?

Many people might say: "But I didn't kill anybody, so why do I need to go to confession? I'm a good person, I help my neighbor, and I'm honest and kind." This may all be true, but there is more to take into consideration than that.

Jesus said: *Whoever has my Commandments and observes them, is the one who loves me* (John 14:21). God has imprinted the substance of the Ten Commandments in your heart and mind; this is natural law. Sin is a refusal to keep God's commandments. Sin is saying to God: *I want to do it my way and not your way.* God's love for you is so great, that He allows you to use your free will even if sometimes you use this gift to turn your back on Him.

Each Commandment encompasses a wide array of things; so, for instance, the fifth Commandment: *Thou shall not kill*, refers not only to committing murder, but also to all injuries to the body or soul, such as anger, hatred, and revenge. Let's take a look at the aspects that each Commandment encompasses:

Examination of Conscience for Teens based on the Ten Commandments:

First Commandment:
I am the Lord your God
- ✝ Did I have false Gods in my life that I gave greater attention to, such as money, drugs, Internet, fame, etc?
- ✝ Did I doubt or deny the existence of God?

✞ Did I believe in something superstitious or engage in a superstitious practice such as palm reading, fortune telling, horoscopes, quija boards, séances, the occult, tarot cards?

✞ Did I love God with all my heart?

✞ Did I receive Holy Communion in the state of mortal sin or without the necessary preparation?

✞ Did I violate the one-hour Eucharistic fast?

✞ Did I put my faith in danger by reading or watching something contrary to Catholic faith and morals?

✞ Did I put my faith in danger by attending meetings or participating in activities organized by organizations that are directly contrary to the Catholic Church, like the free-masons, the communist party, "new age" cults?

Second Commandment:
You shall not take the name of the Lord your God in vain

✞ Did I blaspheme or insult God?

✞ Did I use the name of God carelessly, mockingly, jokingly, angrily or in any other irreverent manner?

✞ Did I keep the promises and resolutions I made to God?

✞ Did I get angry with God?

Third Commandment:
Remember to keep holy the Sabbath day

✞ Did I miss Mass on a Sunday or a Holy Day of Obligation through my own fault?

✞ Did I dress inappropriately for Mass?

✞ Did I arrive late for Mass, or leave early, on purpose?

✞ Did I set aside Sunday as a day of rest and family time? Did I do unnecessary homework?

Fourth Commandment:
Honor your father and your mother

✞ Did I disobey my parents?

✞ Did I neglect to help my parents when help was needed?

✝ Did I treat my parents with the respect and affection that is due to them?

✝ Did I cause tension, arguments and/or fights in my family?

✝ Did I have a disordered desire for independence?

✝ Did I fulfill my family obligations (chores)?

Fifth Commandment:
You shall not kill

✝ Did I easily get angry and loose my temper?

✝ Did I cause harm to anyone with my words or actions?

✝ Did I hold a grudge, refuse to forgive, desire revenge or hate someone who offended me?

✝ Was I envious, impatient, unkind, jealous or hateful towards another?

✝ Did I ask pardon when I offended anyone?

✝ Did I insult, bully or offensively tease others?

✝ Did I kill or physically injure anyone?

✝ Did I attempt suicide?

✝ Did I have an abortion? Did I advise anyone to have an abortion? (One that procures an abortion is automatically excommunicated, as is anyone who is involved in an abortion, Canon 1398)

✝ Did I use birth control pills, whether or not realizing that birth control pills do abort the fetus if and when conceived?

Sixth and Ninth Commandments:
You shall not commit adultery / You shall not covet your neighbor's wife

✝ Did I willfully entertain impure thoughts or desires?

✝ Did I engage in impure conversations? Did I start them?

✝ Did I use impure or suggestive words?

✝ Did I willfully watch impure TV shows and movies, videos, plays?

✝ Did I deliberately look at impure pictures, Internet sites or magazines? Did I read impure materials?

✝ Did I give scandal by dressing immodestly?

✝ Did I engage in acts such as "petting", "necking", passionate kisses, or prolonged embraces that could lead to sin?

✝ Did I commit impure acts by myself (masturbation) or with someone else (premarital sex)?

✝ Did I commit adultery (sex with a married person)?

✝ Did I practice artificial birth control (by pills, device or withdrawal)?

Seventh and Tenth Commandments:
You shall not steal / You shall not covet your neighbor's goods

✝ Did I cheat, deceive or committed fraud?

✝ Did I steal, help or encourage others to steal or keep stolen goods?

✝ Have I made restitution for stolen goods?

✝ Was I envious of my neighbor's goods?

✝ Was I greedy? Do I spend too much money because of vanity, or caprice?

Eight Commandment:
You shall not bear false witness against your neighbor

✝ Did I lie?

✝ Have I unjustly or rashly accused others?

✝ Did I tell lies about other people (calumny)?

✝ Did I gossip or reveal other's faults?

✝ Did I fail to keep a secret that should be confidential?

Concerning the Precepts of the Church:

✝ Did I fast on Ash Wednesday and Good Friday?

✝ Did I eat meat on the Fridays of Lent or Ash Wednesday?

✝ Did I fail to receive Holy Communion during Easter time?

✝ Did I go to Holy Communion in a state of mortal sin? Without fasting (water and medicine permitted) for one hour from food and drink?

✝ Did I make a bad confession?

✝ Did I fail to contribute to the support of the Church?

See the point? Now, some sins are more serious than others. Mortal, or deadly, sin deprives you of sanctifying grace. When you commit a mortal sin, you are spiritually *dead,* you are in total darkness, and you have cut off all communication with God. Did you know that during all the time you remain in mortal sin, all the good works you do, do not earn you any merits for Heaven, and more important, if you die in mortal sin, you forfeit eternal life with God? That's why it's important for you to know the three conditions that are necessary for a sin to be mortal. They are the following:

1. *Grave matter: the thought, desire, word, action or omission must be seriously wrong.*
2. *Full knowledge that what you are about to do is a serious sin*
3. *Full Consent: you do it out of your free will.*

Venial sin is a less serious offense against God, and does not deprive your soul of sanctifying grace, although it weakens your will and lessens your power to resist mortal sin.

Confession is a wonderful Sacrament that reconciles you with God, cleanses your soul and fills you with joy and strength. It is an amazing treasure that we Catholics have!

Once you understand what sin does to your soul, you will surely make a resolution to go to confession more often. Go through the Examination of Conscience above to help you prepare to do a good confession. Always remember that for a confession to be valid, you need to have true contrition – sorrow – for your sins and to have the resolution to not sin again.

Your life is God's gift to you.

What you do with it is your gift back to God.

LaVergne, TN USA
29 September 2009
159318LV00001B/1/P